Farewell to Prague

Farewell to Prague

Miriam Darvas

MP PUBLISHING

Farewell to Prague

First published by MacAdam/Cage Publishing in San Francisco, CA in 2001
This revised edition published in 2015 by
MP Publishing
12 Strathallan Crescent, Douglas, Isle of Man IM2 4NR British Isles
mppublishingusa.com

Original Library of Congress Cataloging-in-Publication Data
Darvas, Miriam, 1926–
    Farewell to Prague / by Miriam Darvas.
    p. cm.
    ISBN: 0-9673701-4-0 (alk. paper)
1. World War, 1939–1945 — Czechoslovakia. 2. World War, 1939–1945 — Personal narratives, Czech. 3. World War, 1939–1945 — Children. 4. World War, 1939–1945 — Europe. 5. Prague (Czech Republic) — History. 6. Refugee children — Czechoslovakia.
I. Title
    D811.5 .D34 2000

ISBN 978-1-84982-243-5
Also available in eBook

The events, situations, and characters herein are all true but are reconstructed from the sometimes imperfect device of memory. Some names have been changed.

For Karen and Lisa

The Sunken City

Like one lost in the fog in the evening,
groping to find that lost road
toward the City,
which yesterday, in the earthquake,
sank into the Bottomless Lake;
but people were expecting him there longingly,
desires, beliefs, goals, and battles,
wife, ecstasy, music, life;
but he doesn't yet know
that all this has been lost beneath the surface;
he just keeps going, or would go, but false sound shadows
lead him astray from the path:
woes, slogans, echoes, songs,
foghorns sounding alarms,
a will-o'-the-wisp, a phantom, a fog mirage;
in the heavy, dense silence that aches in sympathy,
the dark wings of the shadows of fate rustle,
a witch's gloating cackles,
the withering horror of the deaf darkness
gapes, like the throat of execution day,
from its ice caves of distant old age,
a wolf howls, a hyena laughs,
and the dog of death barks:—

Oh, where have you gone, Sunken City?
Oh, where are you, Life, Youth?

János Darvas
(The Author's Father)
1929

The legacy of my past is a dichotomy of two selves. One half of me wants to be here, the other somewhere else. Wherever I am, it is the wrong place for part of me. I straddle two worlds, not fully comfortable in either. I can live anywhere but am at home nowhere. My roots are shallow but they spread like fingers across the globe, encompassing the world.

—Miriam Darvas

1933

Berlin

The muffled tapping of my father's typewriter came through the closed study door. The fir log in the fireplace crackled. I watched it send sparks up the chimney as I listened drowsily to the singsong of my mother's voice reading to my younger sister, Nora. The smell of fresh-baked bread wafted in from the kitchen along with the steady swish-swish sound of Lotte, our housekeeper, as she mopped the hallway. It was dusk on a chilly fall day.

Suddenly, a scream knifed through the air. A voice outside shouted, "Get that Jew." My mother fell silent and raised her head. Her eyes were wide, her lips tight. My father's tapping stopped. I ran to the window.

The red armbands with black swastikas in white circles whipped through the air. Up down, up down flew the truncheons. Black boots danced wildly around a small body on the cobblestones.

I pressed my palms against the windowpanes as if that would ward off the blows. The sound of crunching bone sliced into my head and lodged there like shards of glass. "No, no," I screamed, but no sound came.

Windows across the street were quickly closed and curtains drawn. Doors slammed shut.

Cries weakened into whimpers and then stopped, but the men continued to whip the inert body. At last, they stopped. One of them, his face sweaty, legs apart and hands on hips, stood in a puddle of blood and gazed impassively at the body.

He looked like the posters showing the might of the Storm Troopers. The men stepped over their kill and walked off, swinging their truncheons. Silence covered the street.

Across the street, Mrs. Blumberg opened the window and leaned out. Her hands cupped her mouth, muffling a scream. A moment later she was outside, kneeling, and rocking the limp body.

My parents ran outside and I followed. The acrid smell of blood rose from the pavement and invaded my body. Mother held Mrs. Blumberg in her arms, whispering softly to her. Blood had seeped into her dress and left a ragged stain.

Her wails reverberated from the walls of the silent street and slithered into my bones as an icy chill. The chill grew into a massive obstruction in my stomach that forced itself out in a bitter-tasting mass. As I vomited, my legs gave way under me. The walls converged into an unyielding stretch of red. Everything was blurred. People came running. They looked like gray sticks bending and shouting.

Kurt Blumberg, my seven-year-old schoolmate and first love, was curled in a ball on the street.

My father picked me up and carried me home. I hung limply over his shoulders. Choking hiccups exploded from my lungs and cut off my air. My father stroked my back as I leaned over his shoulder and soaked his shirt with tears. Then I threw up again.

An ambulance came and took Kurt and Mrs. Blumberg away.

The remaining night engulfed me like a black pool. Nora slept peacefully in her bed next to mine, but I could not sleep. I stood at the window and watched Kurt's dormer window across the street, waiting for him to come and lean out. The window stayed closed, reflecting the moon. It had always been open so that we could wave good-night to each other across the rooftops. Now the moon stared back at me like a frozen eye, cold and tearless. I knew then that everything had hopelessly changed.

—

Only months before, my life had been brimful of anticipation. I was going to go to school in the fall and was no longer considered a child. On my birthday in July, I was allowed to join the adults for dinner. The table was gleaming with glass and china. The lace curtains on the windows displayed their intricate pattern of flowers and birds against the dark windowpanes, and warmth radiated from the stove. On my chair was a large cornucopia wrapped in rainbow-colored paper. Filled with candies and cookies, it was a traditional gift given on the first day of school. It was as tall as I was, so that I had to wrap both arms around it in order to hold it. The guests were as dear and as close to me as family. Though they were not relations, I called them my aunts and uncles.

Aunt Moidi was an actress who'd been a smashing success on the stage in Prague. Uncle Lex was a journalist like my father, and his wife, Steffie, was a painter. Then there was Uncle Charles, a newspaper correspondent from America. I adored his stories about New York, where the buildings were so tall one could not see the sky, and about California where the oranges were as big as soccer balls and the sun shined all the time. I had him tell me these stories over and over.

Uncle Egon, a writer, handed me a neatly wrapped package. I tore off the wrapping and was delighted to find a new book by him, autographed and dated 1933. And there was Genia the ballerina, my dancing teacher. Tall and lithe, she had white skin and a head of short curls that sat on her head like woven copper. She was not demanding in her teaching and was soft as down. Every complaint of pain in my toe or ankle or knee was met with a soft hug and an immediate trip to the Café across the street from her studio for ice cream.

She would admonish my father to be less demanding of me, to which he would reply with a silent stare.

It was the last time we would all be together.

Lotte served the soup to begin my school-starting celebration. During the course of the dinner, I sensed raw anxiety in the conversation. The word "Nazi" cropped up several times and

3

reduced the conversation to a whisper, sometimes bringing it to a standstill. Then it was resumed and "Hitler" and "Gestapo" and "Jew" were the words that created a tense hush.

"What is 'Jew?'" I interrupted the conversation with my question.

My father said, "A Jew is a person of a religious belief. Some say Jews are a race. I am a Jew. Steffie is a Jew."

"Am I a Jew?"

"No."

"Why?"

"Because your mother is Catholic."

"Then I am Catholic?"

"You can choose what you want to be."

My father, with a grave inflection, then explained what "Nazi" and "Gestapo" were.

I knew that some ominous threat lurked beyond the security of my own warm room. Something was wrong.

I wanted to open my cornucopia and asked Mother if I could. Father insisted that I finish eating first. I smiled at my mother.

"That child is going to win the world with her smile," Aunt Steffie said.

"Let's hope she will have more to offer than a smile," Father replied. "Eat your soup," he said to me. My father was not won with a smile—which I knew. I folded my arms across my chest challenging him to make me eat. "I don't want to."

Father did not tolerate defiance and ordered me to my room. I knew I could not argue with him. I slid off my chair and grabbed my cornucopia and rushed to the door. Steffie came to open it for me and pushed me through with a hushed, "Quick, go."

I tore open the cornucopia and dumped the contents on my bed. Chocolates, cookies, and candies wrapped in multicolored wrappers shaped into triangles, circles, and stars scattered across the blanket. I sampled most of them and went to bed happy and triumphant.

—

That September, Kurt and I had set off for school, our brief-cases proudly strapped to our backs, looking forward to a wonderful new world of adventure. On the way home, we saw men in brown uniforms and polished boots in groups of four or six walking on the sidewalks. They had red armbands with strange patterns in them, and their shiny boots sounded solid and confident. Kurt said that they were bad men. When I asked why, he said that they didn't like anybody. We were too anxious to get home to continue with the matter. Day after day, we went to school together. After school, we would run across the street to each other's apartments for homework or games. We called to each other across the dormer roofs at night and spent all our weekends together.

Then things started going wrong and I did not understand why.

The day after they killed Kurt, Father did not allow me to go back to school. Though I loved going, I was glad not to have to go out alone. I was afraid of the men in their black boots and their red armbands.

I did my schoolwork at home under my father's impatient tutelage.

The days crept away slowly and silently. Fear and uncertainty hung over the house like a suffocating blanket. Lotte no longer came.

My father was preoccupied. He seemed unaware of us. He paced a lot and wrote endlessly. Sometimes he was gone all night. He was distributing anti-government leaflets, I later learned. My mother's blue eyes became dull and unseeing. She performed her tasks mechanically. Though she tried to console me, I felt she was somewhere else. An impenetrable curtain separated us. I had to spend more time helping around the house and watching Nora. At night I would look at the closed window across the street hoping Kurt would appear and wave, but the window remained shut. I cried myself to sleep.

The only bright day of the week was Saturday, when Mother and I went to the library. For hours I could browse through the stacks of books and read anything I wanted. I liked to read the adventures of the girl called Inge who went to places like Sumatra and Borneo. I loved the story of Tecumseh. When my father went with me to the library, I had to read Voltaire or Dostoyevski, Turgenev or De Maupassant. Though I liked reading their stories, it chafed me that I was forced to read them.

One night, the incessant ringing of the doorbell awakened me. I jumped out of bed quickly when I heard voices. I ran down the stairs, and peeked into the study as I usually did when I wanted to listen to the adults. Uncle Lex was slumped in my father's chair. Mother was dabbing his forehead with a towel. Father paced and nervously lit one cigarette after another.

"Is Uncle Lex hurt?" I asked.

Mother handed the bloody towel to Father and came to lead me back to bed.

"Leave her here. She must learn what these people do," Father said.

"She is too young," Mother protested.

"For her own protection, she must know." I noticed that his hand holding the towel was trembling.

My mother left me standing at the door and took the towel from my father's hand.

Uncle Lex's hands lay limp and misshapen on his thighs. He had been caught distributing anti-Nazi leaflets. They held him for three days and broke every knuckle in his fingers. I did not understand why they had done that.

"I'll be all right," he said. "They're rounding up the clergy, the Communists, and those who oppose the regime. You'd better leave, János. They'll be here for you and your family soon."

The "they" he was talking about must be the men in black boots. The ones who killed Kurt, I thought. I clung to the railing with all my might and bit my lip so that no sound would escape.

"Steffie left for Prague and I'll join her there in a few days. Charles will get me the papers. I think you should leave immediately," Lex said.

My ears buzzed, the room expanded and contracted. My knuckles turned white from holding on to the railing. I did not want to go anywhere.

Mother bandaged Lex's hands and Father took him to Charles's apartment.

My father no longer went out. My mother, who was a professor of languages, stopped going to work. Her blue eyes became opaque and gray. The dimple that formed in her left cheek when she smiled no longer appeared. My father spent hours on the telephone talking in hushed tones. His voice was hollow, his brown eyes dark and angry, and his mouth like a pencil stroke smudged across his face.

A week or so after Lex's nighttime visit, I was, as usual, unable to sleep and watched Kurt's window for some sign of life, even though I knew there would be none. Nora turned on her side and made a strange little cry. I wondered if she was having a nightmare. My parents' voices floated up the stairwell. I tiptoed out of my room, closed the door, and crouched at the head of the stairs.

"We'll have to leave, Tilly," my father was saying. Mother's name was Mathilde, but everyone called her Tilly.

"But where can we go?"

"We'll join Lex and Steffie in Prague."

"When?"

"In a few days. I have to make arrangements."

"We can't just leave on such short notice," Mother said. Father was pacing. "We must."

"I'll pack a few things."

"We're not taking anything."

"But we can't leave everything behind."

Father's tone was impatient. "We can't carry anything. We'll have to cross the border on foot."

I went to my room, cradled my doll, and cried.

The days went by in a haze. I did not know what was happening.

A few days later, Mother gathered a few things and put them in a suitcase. She took the familiar family portrait out of its frame, rolled it into a tube, and put it in her pocket. I took my doll.

Father walked out of the door, I behind him. My mother carried Nora on her hip. She closed the door to our apartment and stood for a while, her shoulders slumped, looking at the house. Then she took me by the hand and we walked across to Mrs. Blumberg's. As soon as I was inside, I began to cry. Mrs. Blumberg and Mother cried and hugged. Mother exhorted Mrs. Blumberg to leave with us. She said she had to stay for her son. She wouldn't leave the place where he was buried. I ran out and sat on the suitcase. My mother came out from Mrs. Blumberg's with a tear-stained face and picked up the suitcase.

"Put it down," my father said.

"It's only a change of clothes."

"You'll be carrying Nora across the border."

Mother reluctantly placed the suitcase on the stairs. She had shrunk into herself and seemed removed from the scene.

Father turned to me. "You cannot take that."

"It's just my doll."

"Leave it."

I clutched it to my chest. "No."

He took the doll from me and placed it on the stairs.

"We'll have to walk a long way."

I picked up my doll and sat on the steps. "But we're going by train."

"Only to the border."

I clutched the doll with fierce protectiveness. "I can carry her."

"Put it back."

He pulled me off the stairs. I resisted.

"I'll get you another."

"Another is not the same."

"Be sensible. It's just a doll."

"It's not just a doll." I clung to her as if my care of her would undo what was happening to us.

Father pulled the doll from my clutching arms and placed her on the stairs next to Mother's suitcase. He took me by the hand and pulled me along. I kept looking back at my doll sitting alone on the stairs. She was all I had left of my almost seven years of life and now I had nothing. I cried all the way to the station.

We waited for some time for the train to arrive. The bench was hard and cold. We finally boarded in late afternoon. I sat by the window. Mother sat between Nora and me, and Father sat opposite. Each clack of the wheels burned a silent cry into my ears and lodged in my head like smoldering cinders—hot, but dead.

Telephone poles zipped by like stick ghosts, their crossbars evil swinging arms reaching for me. Tears gathered behind my eyes and ran down my throat. I felt I would drown in the water pooling in my chest.

I leaned against my mother's shoulder, seeking solace in the soft warmth of her body. The rocking train eased me into a restless sleep. Distorted images of blood, viscous and wet, dripped inside my head. Black boots danced around my inert body. The darkness converged into a sea of blood in which I was drowning. I woke up screaming. My mother's soft voice was consoling and I fell into a half-sleep. Even in this state, my mind would not let go of menacing images. Questions floated through my mind, defying me with their lack of answers. What was this Nazi that could kill without cause? That could make my stoic father falter and my indomitable mother's beautiful face become ashen and drawn? Something I did not understand was beginning to take shape somewhere inside me. It coiled itself around my stomach like a disease. My mother's warmth could not dispel the images or the oppressive coil pressing my insides into a hard ball.

I don't remember how long it took to get to where we were going, but it was getting dark and an early fall rain was coming down in sleety sheets when we stepped off the train. We crossed the railroad tracks. Before us lay the muddy field we had to cross.

"We have to walk across the field to the Czech border. Follow me," Father said.

I did not want to go anywhere. I wanted to lie down in a cozy bed and go to sleep. I hung back and watched my parents slosh through the mud.

"Move, Miriam," Father said. He turned back and took me by the hand.

Wind whipped rain into my face. It beat down like machine gun fire leaving pockmarks in the muddy field. A path led to the footbridge Uncle Charles had described.

"That's the bridge," Father said.

Across the bridge was the Czech border. The Czech guard-house sat at the exit of the bridge. Smoke from its chimney curled over its roof, illuminated by the fire below, lingered briefly like a protective blanket, then melded with the rain. A warm glow shone through the window and formed a puddle of light on the path.

Mother whispered something to Father. The tremor in her voice made my palms sweat. He did not respond but blew into his hands and rubbed them together, then jammed them into his coat pockets.

"Let's go," he said, then turned and, leaning into the slanting rain, pushed across the field, Mother behind him. Nora stumbled along by Mother's side, hanging onto the hem of her coat.

Afraid to move, I watched them weave through the curtain of rain. Rivulets ran down my neck and face. The wind constricted my chest. It snapped the coat hem from Nora's hand. She began to whimper. Mother picked her up and carried her on her hip.

Father looked back and saw me still standing there, huddled in my coat collar.

"Miriam, move!" he said. His voice was low and impatient.

I wrapped my wet scarf tighter around my ears and stuffed the ends into my coat collar. Bracing myself against the wind, I began the slow trek from one puddle to another. The mud oozed into my shoes, my feet sloshed and slid inside. My chest felt like a taut drum.

Father stopped under a tree, but its barren branches offered no protection. We gathered around him.

"You run across the bridge as soon as I get to the river."

"But look at the way it sways. It's not safe," Mother said.

"There's no choice. You just have to do it. I'm going downstream to wade across. I'll meet you at the other side."

"But why?"

"Because women and children are permitted to cross, but men are not."

Afraid that I might lose my father, I said, "I'm going with you."

"You stay with your mother. And don't argue. This is not the time."

I wanted to protest, but reluctantly stayed with Mother. I knew that the situation demanded my obedience.

He again looked in the direction from which we had come. Then we walked on. Mother reached the bridge and Father walked along the bank downstream, looking for a place to wade across. Some distance from where I was standing, he edged into the rushing water.

Rain obscured my vision and dissolved the landscape.

Mother's insubstantial shape floated out onto the wooden bridge.

She stopped. The silhouette of her body shimmered through the rain.

"Come on, Miriam," she shouted into the wind.

Water lapped at her feet and thundered over the bridge.

I was cold, yet I was sweating. Mother was halfway across when she turned again. "Run, Miriam, run." Her voice emanated the tears I knew she was crying. She stood immobile, letting the rain wash over her.

I knew that safety and warmth lay across the swinging rope. "I'm coming," I shouted into the wind, but I was unable to move. As she stumbled across the swaying bridge, Mother held the ropes with one hand and clutched Nora with the other. She reached the guard's hut. An orange shaft of light broke the darkness as the door opened and briefly framed her there. She was now in Czechoslovakia and I was still glued to German soil. A few feet of ground and a swinging bridge lay between me and safety.

"Miriam." Mother's cry lingered in the air. The orange pool of light promised safety. I took a reluctant step onto the bridge.

Suddenly floodlights lit up the scene. My shadow, distorted by the rain, stood before me.

"Halt!" someone shouted from behind me. My heart pounded. My arms were seized and I was dragged backward through the mud and flung into the back of a panel truck.

I scrambled off the floor of the truck and jumped out. The soldier who had thrown me in took me by the collar and tossed me back inside. Defeated by the soldier's superior strength, I turned around and put my hands under my armpits to warm them, but I could not stop shivering. Through the door, I saw two other soldiers farther downstream. Their rifles were aimed at my father. He was standing up to his neck in the rushing river with his hands raised over his head.

The soldier who was guarding me pranced around the mud.

"Mach schnell," he shouted toward the river. "Mir ist kalt," he mumbled to himself.

I was cold, too. I was covered with mud thick as clay.

"Get out and keep your hands up," one soldier said, his rifle still pointed at my father's head. My father waded to shore and the two soldiers prodded him into the truck with their rifles. They climbed in and sat on the bench opposite us.

The door clanked shut. The driver waded around to the front and the van lurched forward. One of the guards gave me a tentative smile. I looked away.

The truck bounced over the muddy field and jostled the bodies of guard and prisoner alike. Only the rifles, placed firmly between the guards' legs, were solidly anchored to the floorboards.

The soldiers lit cigarettes. The one with the tentative smile offered one to my father. He shook his head. The smoke drifted through the mesh window and disappeared into the rain. Puddles formed around the men's feet. The floorboards creaked. Father shivered as water dripped down his face. He had taken off his shoes when he went into the river and his wet socks were making pools around his feet.

The truck stopped with a lurch. The driver opened the door and the soldiers pushed us out. We entered a stone building with iron doors flanking a long corridor. At the end of the hall was an open door. The soldiers brought us inside and slammed the solid door behind us.

A plank suspended from one wall by two iron chains served as a cot. On the wall opposite were three more small planks, also suspended by iron chains, serving as table and chairs. Wind whistled through a barred window. A bulb, protected by wire mesh, dangled overhead and gave off a dull glow. In the corner between the cot and the door was a dirty toilet.

Father leaned against the wall. I huddled on the cot. My body was clammy and my mouth quivered with cold. Wet and exhausted, I was only dimly aware of him sliding to the floor. His chin slumped onto his chest. His arms lay limply on the floor palms up. He looked like a puppet whose strings had been let go. Water dripped from his clothes and formed a puddle under him. Through the small, square window high in the wall I watched the clouds change from gray to black.

A peephole in the door opened.

"Stand up," said a menacing voice.

Father gave no sign of having heard the order. I jumped off the cot and pulled him up, but his knees buckled under him. Sweat poured from every pore in my body.

The door burst open and two men in black boots stomped in, prodded him in the stomach with truncheons, and forced him up against the wall. Unable to protect himself from the rhythmic blows now falling on him, he slid back down. The smoldering something uncoiled itself, raced through my veins, and exploded into a roar in my ears. My foot shot out and connected with a black boot. "Leave my father alone!" I shouted and clung to the arm that was about to deliver another blow. The arm shot back and hurled me against the wall. My teeth slammed together. A warm liquid trickled down my chin. The room swam, then vanished.

I came to on the cot. My jaw and head hurt. There was a bleeding gash on Father's forehead and one eye was swollen shut. I did not understand why we were here, why my father was beaten. Nothing made sense. I wanted to say something, but no words came.

From far away I heard Father whisper hoarsely, "I'm proud of you." His voice was caressing. I felt a flush of pride.

The following morning, the same two soldiers from the day before opened the cell door. One grabbed me under the arms and pulled me through the door. The other put his rifle butt in my father's back and pushed him forward.

"Be brave," Father whispered as we were led out of the cell.

"Let me go," I cried, but the hands clamped around my arms more firmly.

I could not stop the fear that chilled every bone in my body, but then something inside me snapped as it had in the cell the day before, and I kicked and squirmed and tried to bite the hand cupped under my left shoulder but could not quite reach it.

I kept looking back, and glimpsed my father tripping with each push of the soldier's rifle. The soldier did not relax his grip on my arm. I used my feet as brakes as he dragged me across the floor that offered no resistance.

"Where are we going?" I asked the guard who had smiled at me.

He gave me a vague look.

The room we were led to was another cell, furnished with a desk, two chairs, and what looked like a sun lamp. Behind the desk sat a young, blond, pale-faced man. His black uniform and his features seemed to have been stamped from a perfect mold and were so stiff that I thought he would crack if he bent over or if he smiled. His hands were flat on the table. The swastika in its white circle on a red band on his upper left arm screamed a warning.

The soldiers pushed us onto the chairs and remained standing behind us.

"Papers," said the pale-faced man.

Father handed him the papers Uncle Charles had given him.

The man looked at them, turned them over and turned them over again. He looked at my father.

"What's your name?" he asked.

With composure and certainty my father replied, "Johann Muller." Muller was my mother's maiden name.

I quickly looked at the floor.

"Where were you born?"

"Berlin," he lied. He had been born in Budapest.

I kept my eyes glued to a knot in a plank on the floor.

"What were you doing at the border?"

"We were on our way to visit the children's grandmother."

I did not know my grandmother and was surprised to hear that I might have one after all.

"You, girl, what's your name?"

I was still concentrating on the knot in the floor, while holding on to the edge of the chair with both hands. My ears were buzzing so that I was not aware that the question was asked of me.

The soldier behind me nudged me in the back. "Answer the question."

Tightening the grip on the chair, I looked up into that expressionless face. My mind went blank. "What question?" My voice shook.

The stiff man drummed his fingers on the table impatiently. "What's your name?" His voice was acrid smoke. It curled around me like a whip.

"Muller," I lied too, hoping my answer sounded real.

"Where were you born?"

"Cologne." Not having time to form a lie, I told the truth.

He stared at me. I was tempted to lower my eyes, but held firm.

Suddenly his hand moved up into the air and with a quick motion he said, "Take them back."

I thought we had not passed the test. My palms were wet, my legs weak as we were led to the exit.

The truck was backed up to the building. Its metal door opened at me. My heart raced. Where were they taking us? Father's hand clamped mine like a vise. The two men nudged Father into the van. The one with the vague smile lifted me into the van, then climbed in behind me. The door slammed. The other went to the driver's seat. We sat on the planks in silence and I clung to Father's arm. The vehicle lurched forward and rolled and bounced over the mud and the puddles. It was dark, but a sliver of light rose gray on the horizon.

The fear of what lay ahead choked the breath out of me. I had no control over my trembling body. My mouth and head hurt. I gasped for air.

My father struggled to pull a handkerchief from his wet pants pocket. He handed it to me. "Here, wipe your mouth." His tone was unusually gentle.

The act of wiping my face brought back my breath, and my body stopped trembling. The landscape unreeled in reverse from yesterday's drive. The van stopped some distance from the bridge. It had stopped raining. The driver came around the side of the van and unlocked the cage.

The soldier sitting next to me jumped out. I remained glued to my seat.

"Austeigen." He seemed to be making a request.

Certain that we were going to be shot, I pushed myself against the back of the seat, hoping to become invisible. The soldier stepped inside and lifted me out. I pummeled his head with my fists. He put me down, held my hands together, and said, "You can go." His rifle remained hanging by his side. Father jumped out.

"Go. Go." The soldier waved his arms, then slammed the door. He walked to the front of the van. About to slide behind the wheel, he turned and shook his finger at us. "If we find you here tomorrow, you'll be imprisoned permanently." He disappeared behind the wheel.

Without waiting for him to crank the engine, my father and I ran across the field. The bridge held no terror for me now. The water still lapped at it, but I floated across it with winged feet. Mother was standing in the open door of the guard's hut. I fell into her arms.

I tried to tell her what had happened, but tears were choking my words. She stepped away from me and stood silent and immobile, watching me as if through a veil. Wet drops hung in the corner of her lids. I felt her pain. It hissed and curled in the very walls of my veins, gurgling in my throat like bitter water.

When the blackness of the night turned into a gray dawn, I fell asleep on a cot in the guard's hut.

Toward evening we were on the train. Rain sheeted against the windows. I leaned against my mother's shoulder for comfort. The clack-clack rhythm of the wheels rocked me to sleep. When I awoke, we had arrived in Prague.

1933 — 1939

Prague

As quickly as the terror began, it ended. Or so it seemed at the time. We found a beautiful flat in Prague. I immediately felt at home there. My parents soon made a new life for themselves. My mother's blue eyes were no longer sad and my father was relaxed. During the day, I would think of Kurt's closed window, a black eye staring at me accusingly. I cried myself to sleep and my dreams were nightmarish. My mother worried about my being so thin. She said my eyes were too large and dark in my thin face.

Father bought me a new doll for my birthday, but I did not want it. It was not the same as the one I had left and, besides, I did not want anything I might have to part with again.

Soon I met Angelika and had a new friend. Winter fell and then came spring.

The white, upright blossoms of the chestnut trees lining the boulevards glowed like candles among the dark green leaves of their crowns. From the old cobblestone streets, the city's ancient churches rose toward the heavens, their gilded cupolas glistening in the sun. The river Vltava meandered through the city, dividing the Old Town from the New.

In the Old Town were the bustling marketplaces that had been there since time began. In the New Town were cultivated parks and elegant homes. On a hill, towering majestically above it all, stood Hradcany, the castle of the kings of Bohemia and in modern times the home of Tomas Garrigue Masaryk, founder and first president of Czechoslovakia. After World War I, Czechoslovakia was created out of parts of Germany, the Sudetenland (a mountainous region between Bohemia and Silesia), and parts of Hungary populated by Czechs and Slovaks.

Masaryk married Charlotte Garrigue, an American, and took her maiden name as his middle one. People loved his American marriage and were always proud to be connected to America through their president. I would often see him ride through the streets of Prague on his black horse, unaccompanied by guards. Crowds would line the streets and cheer this distinguished, slender gentlemen wearing his metal-rimmed glasses and a neat goatee. I would cheer along.

When my father was away on an assignment, my mother and my sister, Nora and I would spend Sundays exploring the city. Sometimes we would sit on a bench by the river and watch the flotsam whipping down the river Vltava. Sometimes we walked the narrow, winding streets leading to the castle to look down on the city, and sometimes we played in the sandbox in Riegrove Sady. During my holidays from school, I liked best to go shopping with my mother and stroll through the market square in the Old Town. Yellow, blue, and green canvas umbrellas covered the stands and threw round shadows onto the cobblestones.

Mother chose vegetables, cheese, and flowers from the stalls. I skipped along, keeping up with her brisk walk. Her long blond braid was always wound around her head like a crown. I was proud of my blue-eyed mother, with her dainty nose, and her translucent skin and the dimple in her left cheek. I liked the admiring way people looked at her.

I loved the markets. The stalls were filled with colorful foods. The multicolored umbrellas shading the stalls and walks were like holiday balloons floating above my head.

The peasants hawking their wares had walked a long way to carry their goods to the market, and those who had no stools sat on their haunches, their produce fanned out on blankets or paper. Their animated voices and brilliant costumes gave the market the atmosphere of a fair.

Mother picked the fruit and vegetables, pointing at the ones she wanted with a delicate finger. The farmer's wife shaped newspaper into cones and dropped the chosen fruit in carefully. By the end of the morning, Mother's net shopping bag would be full of paper cones. I carried the flowers. The market smelled fruity. The sun parched the umbrellas and the smell of vinegar wafted out of the pickle barrels.

An old peasant always sat at one corner of the marketplace in front of his pickle barrel. I liked to go there and fish out the largest pickle. He wrapped it in paper and I gave him my twenty hellers, ran to catch up with Mother, and munched happily on the pickle.

Squatting next to him, his fat wife with her colorful peasant skirt spread across her lap cradled rounds of yellow goat cheese. She stretched out her hand, holding one of her cheeses for sale. Sometimes Mother bought one.

I looked forward to the spring festivals. People danced in the streets to the resounding Czech oom-pah-pah music. Sometimes I walked on the sidewalk holding Mother's hand, keeping pace with the parade of people in national costumes. They wore crowns of flowers with ornamental streamers flowing on the air like opening blossoms. Their full skirts swished as they danced, and their embroidered vests flashed in the sun. The music drifted into the air as vibrant and varied as the balloons that floated up, up into the sky, their strings wiggling like tails.

In the winter we went to the library and spent hours in the stacks choosing books to take home in our net bags.

Often we met Lex and Steffie at the Café Kotva. Lex's fingers had healed, but they were bent like claws. He had to hold his cup of coffee in the hollow of his hands.

Steffie was beautiful. She had green eyes and thick chestnut hair. Often she brought me gifts. She had given me a diary to practice my writing. On my birthdays she always gave me a bouquet of roses, one for each year I had lived. I loved her dearly.

I thought that Lex was too serious to be paired with Steffie's friendly and optimistic nature. He seldom smiled and paid little attention to me, but he was always there when Father was away on a writing assignment. Lex stopped by daily, made certain all was going well, and sometimes even patted me on the head.

The Café Kotva was situated at the entrance to a cul-de-sac, a horseshoe-shaped street on which several foreign embassies sat. Red and white checked curtains hung from rods, covering the lower half of the Kotva's windows. Along the walls, snapped into wooden handles, hung foreign-language newspapers—every language except German. Mr. Zelezny, the proprietor, made it known that German newspapers were not allowed.

The Kotva was famous for its coffees, pastries, and inexpensive food. A blue haze of cigarette smoke drifted around the lamps. Émigrés consumed gallons of coffee and held heated discussions.

Zelezny was a ruddy-faced Czech with a long mustache that he twisted and pulled while chatting with his customers. Around his big belly he wore a butcher's apron on which he kept wiping his hands. Grease and catsup and gravy stained his apron. When he laughed his body shook and the stains wobbled like jelly. He knew that many of his customers were illegal immigrants, but he never mentioned it.

Angelika, my new friend, often came with us to the Café. She lived in the apartment across the landing. We spent most of our free time together, sharing our homes and parents. Angelika's father was also a journalist.

We walked to school together and dawdled our way home together. Sometimes we watched the fifteenth-century clock in the Old Town Square announce the hour. The Twelve Apostles appeared in its rotating windows. We never tired of the display. Angelika also went along with us to the market and the library.

—

Months and months. Then one day, Father announced that I was going to boarding school. I did not want to leave. I liked the writers and artists who stayed for coffee and argued about the meaning of life and discussed politics. I liked the cigarette smoke curling to the ceiling in the living room and the smell of coffee brewing. I liked the lace curtains dancing in the breeze that whispered through the open windows in spring. In winter, I watched frost stars form on the windowpanes while the tile stove radiated warmth. I had begun to have a sense of permanence.

Father had decided that I would be better protected in a remote village. Many of his friends were writers from Germany, and as they escaped to Prague, they brought stories about the intolerable situation for those who resisted the regime. A Nazi party had formed in the Sudetenland, creating unrest and demanding annexation by Germany. With each new refugee came more horror stories. Father feared the Germans might march into Prague. The black uniforms and the red bands with the swastika were casting their shadow over my life again.

"You'll be safer in the country," he told me.

"I don't want to be safe in the country."

"You'll like it there. It's a coeducational boarding school."

"What's that?"

"A school for boys and girls."

"I won't know anyone there."

"You will meet students from other parts of Europe and make new friends."

"I don't want new friends."

"Angelika is going."

"I don't care. I want to stay here."

"You can come home on weekends."

Though that made the prospect of boarding school more palatable, it did not diminish my unhappiness.

Angelika and I went to boarding school under protest. While Father drove us there, I complained and tried to convince him to turn around and forget the school.

"I'm not going to like it there," I said.

"Me neither," said Angelika.

"You'll get used to it."

"I don't want to get used to it. It's going to be awful."

As it turned out, it was awful.

On one of my weekend visits home, Mother and I arrived at the Kotva several minutes early for our meeting with Lex and Steffie. We were sitting by the window, Mother's favorite place, which Zelezny always reserved for us. Mother was impatient and kept moving the curtain aside. Zelezny brought the coffee. Mine was half milk heaped with whipping cream. I usually ended with a white mustache that Zelezny would wipe away with his apron, adding another stain to his collection.

"Waiting for Lex and Steffie?" he asked.

"They're late. I hope they're all right." Mother's voice sounded uncertain.

"The news is terrible. Those goddam Germans. Taking over Austria as if they had the right. They try anything here and we'll blast them to hell."

Mother looked doubtful.

When Lex and Steffie arrived, Zelezny was there immediately with coffee. Lex straddled the chair, resting his arm on the back of it and looking serious. Steffie, silent and tense, sat between Mother and me. She put her arm around me and I snuggled up to her. I could feel her tension.

Lex shifted in his chair. "I think this is going to get worse."

"How much worse?" Mother's voice was so low I could barely hear her.

"The Germans claim the Sudetenland is theirs. I think that might be their next move."

"Where do we go from here?" Mother said.

"If the situation gets worse, Steffie and I are planning to go to France. I think you ought to get Miriam out of school. János and you should be prepared to leave with us."

I listened to this conversation with a growing sense of unease. The memory of what had happened to Kurt returned in waves of nausea. I pushed away the coffee without even touching the luscious mound of whipped cream on top.

"It won't be long before the Germans march into Prague. We have to get out. I heard the Underground is organizing children's transports to England."

"I won't part with my children." Mother's panicked voice made me fight back tears.

"I think you should get the girls out as quickly as possible. I can find out about the transport."

"I can't send the girls away without knowing where they'll be."

"You have to choose."

I squirmed on my seat and snuggled closer into Steffie's arm. I could not imagine going alone across borders.

"How can I send my daughters to possible capture?"

"If they stay here, it will be certain death. You know that. It will be easier for us to get out once the girls are safe."

"But they may not get to England."

"That's a chance you'll have to take."

"I can't take that chance."

I sensed my mother's despair and wished Father were here. He was in Bratislava working at the *Magyar Hirlat*, a Hungarian magazine.

"I'm not leaving," I said firmly, wanting to reassure my mother.

Mother gave me a sad smile. Lex ignored me.

Steffie, who was usually open and gregarious, sat stiff and silent. Mother knotted and unknotted her handkerchief.

That evening Mother drove me back to school. The streets of Prague seemed more silent than usual. Fear hung over me like a shroud.

The teachers and pupils in school were functioning in a haze of uncertainty. I had been placed in Obermeier's history class. He was from the Sudetenland. He spoke Czech only when he felt compelled to explain something to what he perceived to be a blockheaded Czech student. In spite of my fear of him,

I grinned behind my cupped hand whenever he spoke Czech with his ripping German R.

He always carried a birch rod. Like a fencer skewering his opponent, he would pin the object of his disdain to the seat with the point of the birch in the pupil's chest.

"Dieser Dummkopf," he would say, "has not learned the language of culture."

He was a tall, athletic man with blue eyes that glittered like chips of glass. He was handsome in a cruel way. I had believed handsome people to be gentle. Obermeier cured me of that belief.

When he entered the classroom, we had to stand at attention and shout, "Good morning, Herr Obermeier!" Had he been headmaster, we would have been shouting, "Heil Hitler!"

He did not allow us to sit until he had slipped into his black robe, which he always left hanging on the coat rack by the window. He hooked his thumbs into the fold of his robe, clicked his heels, and spat out, "Sit!"

Feet shuffled, chairs scraped, books dropped.

"Silence."

He had a disconcerting way of stalking the aisles, swishing his birch rod like a whip, while his black robe billowed behind him ominously. I hated him with the raw passion of fear.

I was anticipating the coming weekend. Mother was taking me to the theater to see *Emil and the Detectives* in celebration of my twelfth birthday. I looked forward to the respite from the rules and hostilities of school. Angelika would be there.

Chris promised to come. Whenever we were together, I felt a joy I could not explain. His eyes were so dark. When he looked at me, I felt myself melt. After weeks of my sitting next to him in class and trying to make myself noticed, he finally asked me to go to the library with him. I accepted before he had finished the sentence. We held hands, took walks, and studied together. Whenever I had house arrest for an infraction of some stupid rule, Chris would climb out of the boy's dorm, creep along the ledge and jump into my room. We would play chess, and sometimes we would climb out the window and run down to the pond. There we sat holding hands and talking about what we would do when we grew up. I knew I was going to be a journalist like my father. Chris was not certain yet whether he was going to be a lawyer or an architect. When the dinner bell rang, we ran back. I climbed back through my window and Chris sauntered into the dining room.

It was going to be a marvelous birthday party.

I had been in this school long enough to have learned not to show my feelings. I had learned all the unwritten laws of the little jungle.

The school had once been an old, drafty castle. Now it was an old, drafty, coeducational boarding school named Stast, which connoted good luck. It was in the small village of Msec, thirty miles west of Prague. As was traditional in private Czech schools, classes were conducted in German.

Obermeier's guttural voice came from the podium.

I pictured myself sitting beside my mother in the backseat of the car watching the bright green firs and meadows blooming with yellow daisies pass on the drive to Prague. I was anxious for the week to be over and hardly heard Obermeier slap his desk with his birch.

"I am an Aryan," he said with pride and conviction. He was writing "Aryan" on the blackboard, underlining the word emphatically, but the chalk broke on the second stroke. He found another piece of chalk and underlined the word three more times.

I dutifully entered the word in my notebook, and resumed doodling, thinking of Prague, wishing Angelika and I were still walking to and from school there.

There was nothing but harsh rules at Stast. Regardless of its name, the school had never brought me much luck, and Obermeier made my life hell.

Half daydreaming, half asleep, I faintly heard Obermeier step from the podium. I looked up. He was advancing toward me in measured steps. His black robe flapped behind him like bats' wings. My pleasant thoughts vanished. Every muscle in my body tightened. As he came closer, I held my breath. He stopped in front of me and smiled his perfectly even smile. He flexed his birch rod. Without warning he slammed the birch down on my desk. It bounced off my exercise book. I jumped in my seat. My pencil rolled out of my hand and landed at Obermeier's right foot. He kicked it away. In a frightened trance I watched it roll under my desk.

"What is an Aryan?" he asked in his staccato German, his nose in my face.

His glittering pupils stared at me. I stared back. I tightened my muscles in anticipation of the birch. My pulse raced.

"I don't know."

"As usual, you paid no attention."

I remained silent. Once Obermeier had a notion, even if it were false, denial or contradiction would make things worse.

"Well, did you?"

I said nothing and looked at my desk.

"Answer my question!"

I had forgotten what the question had been and asked in a small voice: "Answer which question?" I looked at his puckered lips to avoid his eyes.

"Your defiant—" the last word was lost to me as the birch bit into my shoulder. The pain ran clear down to my feet. My eyes filled with involuntary tears. I bit my lip. Stunned by such hostility, frightened and angry at the same time, I stood and faced Obermeier on shaky legs. My hands clenched into fists, stiffly hugging the seam of my skirt.

"What is an Aryan?" he asked, enunciating each word as if he were talking to a deaf person.

Suddenly he turned and pinned Angelika, who sat next to me, to her seat with the point of the birch.

"What is an Aryan?" he asked again.

Angelika's eyes and mouth opened, but only a sigh escaped her lips.

Obermeier's nose wrinkled with disdain. "Another Czech."

I turned to defend my friend, and as I did, I accidentally knocked the birch from Obermeier's hand.

"She's German," I said, ignoring the fallen birch.

Obermeier's eyes turned to steel. He pointed to the birch on the floor.

"Pick it up," he said between his teeth.

My spine fused. I was not able to move, nor was I able to unglue myself from his hypnotic stare.

Otto, in the row ahead of me, slid out of his seat and with a bow and a shaking hand picked up the birch and handed it to Obermeier, who snatched the rod from Otto's hand.

Otto had arrived at school the day I was conjugating "amo, amas, amat" for Miss Prazakova. He had knocked on the door.

"Who is it?" Miss Prazakova had asked in her high-pitched voice.

"Me," squeaked a falsetto.

"Come in."

The door opened and there stood Otto waiting to be invited to enter.

Miss Prazakova waved him in. "Come in, come in. You're holding up the class."

The new boy swaggered into class in a Hitler Youth uniform: black short pants, brown shirt, black tie, a buckle on his belt with an HJ insignia on it standing for Hitler Jugend, and a leather strap across his right shoulder that I thought was there to hold up his pants. In spite of his regalia he looked crumpled. His white knee socks were inching toward his ankles, and his shirt and pants were wrinkled. This squirt belonged to the master race. I took an instant dislike to him.

Miss Prazakova pointed him to the seat across the aisle from mine. As he passed, Chris tripped him. Otto fell face down and whimpered into the floor. There was the hero sniveling on the floor. Laughter filled the class.

"Get up," Miss Prazakova said.

Otto stood and pointed his finger at Chris.

"He did it. He tripped me."

"Come to the podium." Miss Prazakova looked at him with disdain. He stood before her at attention, looking ridiculous with his sagging socks. Her eyes narrowed and she snapped the strap across his shoulder and frowned. We pounded our desks approvingly.

"Silence." Miss Prazakova tapped her desk with her pencil with one hand and with the other held Otto's leather shoulder strap.

"This is an academic institution, not a political arena. Go and change your clothes, and do not come to my classroom in that outfit again."

She gave him a push. Otto provoked spasms of laughter as he walked to the door. Before he closed the door, he shook his fist at Chris.

A wave of applause had followed Otto out the door. Miss Prazakova could not get our attention for the rest of Latin class.

Now Obermeier was standing over me. I stared at my desk. I tried to figure out just what had gone wrong. Angelika slid down on her bench. The class was silent. I did not see Obermeier raise his arm again. Like a snake's fang the birch bit into my shoulder. I placed my hand on the desk to support my buckling knees.

Angelika whimpered in sympathy and stared at Obermeier like a hypnotized rabbit.

Tucking the birch rod under his armpit, Obermeier gripped my elbow. I struggled to free myself, but his hand tightened. The more I struggled, the firmer the grip became. He marched me to the podium, took me by the shoulders, and forced me to face the class.

"Stretch out your hand," he said.

I was transfixed. My mind did not want to obey the order.

"You're going to have to learn to *parieren*." He stressed the German word.

"Knuckle under." My whole being resisted the idea of knuckling under.

He was furiously snapping the birch like a whip. There was the sound of air being sucked in as the class watched, mesmerized by the confrontation.

Obermeier yanked my hand out and forced it palm up.

"This will teach you to pay attention."

He came down full force on the palm of my hand. The sting of the pain brought tears to my eyes. I instinctively withdrew my hand.

"You dare remove your hand? Put it up at once."

I did not move. I bit my lower lip and swallowed my tears.

Obermeier grabbed my hand again and held it firmly. Wide-eyed, tears blurring my vision, I locked my elbow into my waist and supported my outstretched right hand with my left clamped around my wrist. My brimming eyes focused on Obermeier's glittering pupils. With deliberate force he brought the birch down again. It hissed through the air and bit into my hand.

"One," he counted. I tried to pull my hand away but could not escape his grip.

"For each attempt to remove your hand you will get one more lash," he said, and brought the birch whistling down.

"Two."

I stared at him through a haze of tears, biting my lip till I tasted blood. Wanting to best him, I did not let go of his eyes.

Obermeier hesitated. I thought I saw, his arresting blue eyes turn a soft gray. His grip loosened. My eyes remained solidly fixed on his. He let go of my hand. A collective sigh escaped from the class. The change was too swift for me to grasp immediately, but I realized I had bested him. I did not let go of his eyes.

"Go to your seat," he said and turned to the blackboard.

My hand was on fire. I slid into my seat and blew on it. The cool breath soothed the welts forming on my palm.

"An Aryan is a superior human being of the German race," Obermeier intoned, emphasizing the seriousness of his statement by drumming out each word against the blackboard with his birch.

Angelika's warm hand cautiously touched mine under the desk.

Later, when everything had changed irrevocably, I would remember my triumph over Obermeier. But at that moment, all I could think about was the coming weekend.

My twelfth birthday party turned out to be the last good memory for a long time. My mother, Nora, Angelika, Chris, and I sat on the Letna, a park rising on a hill overlooking the city. We ate ice cream and drank cocoa with whipped cream. As if celebrating my birthday with us, the city band played in the round gazebo, and the park was full of people walking, dancing, and drinking coffee in the warm July sun. It was a beautiful summer. The only cloud on my horizon was having to face Obermeier again.

Farewell to Prague

The March snows had covered the earth so completely that not a patch of green broke through the stark white cover.

We were listening to the radio in Obermeier's class. An announcer was warning in ominous tones of the imminent doom of Czechoslovakia.

Herr Obermeier was from the Sudetenland and referred to it as Sudeten Germany. Perhaps he had a point, since France and Britain had compelled Czechoslovakia to cede the Sudetenland to Germany the year before.

"We will begin our history lesson." Obermeier drew a rough map of Czechoslovakia on the blackboard, leaving out Sudetenland. "You have been taught to believe that Sudeten Germany is Czech territory."

"It was till Germany occupied it," Chris said.

"You have been misinformed."

"By whom?"

Obermeier stepped from the podium. His robe whipped a breeze into my face as he marched past me to the last row, where Chris sat.

"How dare you question my authority?"

"I just made a statement of fact."

The birch whipped through the air and smacked across Chris's shoulder. Chris did not flinch. At the same moment that Obermeier raised his birch the second time, the door flew open and Mr. Kovac, the Czech headmaster, appeared. Obermeier's arm paused in the air. Mr. Kovac walked with funeral steps to the podium. Obermeier lowered his birch.

"Yes?" he asked the headmaster in a patronizing tone of voice. Mr. Kovac ignored him and stepped onto the podium. He cleared his throat. We sat in tense silence.

"Assemble in the library..." Mr. Kovac began, but his voice broke.

Obermeier stood in the aisle with a crooked grin on his face. "Go on," he coaxed Mr. Kovac.

With as much authority as he could muster in the face of Obermeier's scorn, Mr. Kovac added, "At once!"

He stepped off the podium and quickly slipped through the open door.

Without waiting for permission, the students rushed through the door, leaving Obermeier standing at the door in a state of frustrated authority.

I slid out of my desk and ran for the door.

"Darvas, stop." His birch whipped the air. His dangerous voice made me hesitate. What had I done now? Energized by fear and courage, I held my breath and shot past him. His arm reached out, but grabbed only air. I ran down the hall to the library all the while looking behind me fully expecting to see the black robe chasing me. I charged into the library out of breath.

Mr. Kovac mounted the podium, wrapped his robe around him like a shroud, and folded his arms across his chest as if he were in pain. He cleared his throat with a cough. "The Germans are marching into Prague," he said in a voice a pitch higher than usual. "They will probably be here tomorrow."

The silence in the room was so complete that I could hear the whisper of the snow against the double-paned windows.

"The school will close tomorrow," he continued. His hands fluttered in the air like aimless pigeons. He cleared his throat again. "You will have to find your way home alone and..."

His voice trailed off. He pulled out a white handkerchief from the recesses of his cloak and wiped his brow. He was unable to continue speaking and turned to Miss Machulova, the librarian. He whispered something to her, then hurried down the aisle, pushed open the door, and left it ajar. His black robe billowed behind him as he fled down the hall.

Miss Machulova took the headmaster's place on the podium and wrung her hands. Tears streamed down her round face.

"Will the bus take us to Prague?" someone asked.

"There is no transportation," Miss Machulova said. "As Mr. Kovac explained, you'll have to find your way home as best you can."

Whispers swept through the room like a soughing wind.

"Can't we wait for our parents to pick us up?" someone said.

"There's no time. You must gather up your belongings and take what you can."

Miss Machulova had somehow managed to control herself. She rummaged for a handkerchief in her skirt pocket.

"But I can't wade through that snow," Angelika announced with an unusual display of assertiveness.

"I'm afraid you're going to have to. The school will close tomorrow morning." Miss Machulova found her handkerchief, and blew her nose.

"Now go to your rooms and get ready." She stepped from the podium and turned her face away. Her shoulders were shaking, and I knew she was crying again.

The students fled the library as if it were on fire. I watched Miss Machulova methodically gather up books. The dark shadows under her eyes were deep purple. She was startled when she noticed me.

"Get out of here as early as you can tomorrow morning," she said. "And don't carry anything. The snow will slow you and baggage will be a burden."

"Good-bye." I tried to shake her hand.

"Go, go." She gave me a push, then wiped her tears with the sleeve of her blouse.

The hall was pandemonium. The tile floor echoed with the thunder of students crisscrossing to the dorms. Doors slammed, voices rose. Some pupils stood against the walls and cried.

I wondered how we were to get to Prague. I had no idea which direction to go or how long it would take to get there. When I reached the room, Angelika was packing.

"No classes tomorrow," she said cheerfully.

The thought did not cheer me.

"Do you know how to get to Prague?" she asked.

"No, do you?"

"We'll just have to follow the road."

"There is no road. The snow has covered everything."

She shrugged her shoulders and threw an armful of clothing into her suitcase. Blouses, socks, underwear left a trail from drawers to suitcase.

"Miss Machulova said not to take anything."

Angelika ignored me. She bounced on her bulging suitcase, but the lid refused to meet the locks. She yanked out a few clothes and threw them on the floor, then tried to close her suitcase again, but still it would not close. I sat on the bed and watched.

"Forget it. You won't be able to drag it through the snow anyway."

Her hand on her forehead, Angelika pondered the problem.

"I know what we can do. We can put on several pairs of everything." Her face was one big grin.

"Good idea."

We put on several pairs of socks, underwear, two skirts, and two sweaters each. Swaddled in clothes, we sat on our beds and watched the falling snow. It shimmered like tiny lights in the shroud of darkness.

"No more Obermeier." Angelika smiled, trying to cheer me up.

I did not feel consoled. From time to time I dozed, but it was a restless sleep filled with nightmares.

When the morning bell pealed, I jumped out of bed. It was still dark outside and snow was falling.

Angelika struggled into her boots, but could not get them on over the three layers of socks. She peeled off a pair. My arms were so tightly wedged into the sleeves of my coat I could not move. Angelika had to pull it off me so that I could take off a sweater.

The noise of running feet on the tile floor was familiar because we always had early morning calisthenics, but today, the sound was different. Today, it sounded like people fleeing an enemy.

Angelika and I waited till the rush was over and then walked down the empty hall. The teachers' exit was at the opposite end of the students'. The double door was wide open and the teachers pushed one another through the door and disappeared behind a curtain of snow.

Miss Machulova stood at the open oak door at the pupils' exit, key in hand. Snow clung to her clothing like feathers. It hung on her eyelashes and formed a soft mound around her feet like goose down. It reminded me of a pillow fight I'd had with Angelika. The pillows had burst and their contents had clung to our clothing and hair, and drifted into piles around our feet.

"Come on, girls. I have to lock up."

Obermeier casually walked through the teachers' exit. He was the last one out and swaggered through the snow swinging his leather suitcase to the rhythm of unheard drums. He walked past us without a word. I noticed a small smile of triumph at the corner of his mouth.

The dark landscape turned to a light gray in a barely discernible dawn. Pines flanking the road appeared like menacing giants. Their branches, bent with the snow's weight, seemed poised to snap. Snow came down in wads of cotton and lay in four-foot drifts along the ditches.

A slow stream of people, their faces muffled in scarves, slid and shuffled their way along the icy road. People kept to the shoulders of the road and some walked in the ditches. Many dragged suitcases. Mothers pushed baby carts and fathers carried children on their backs. Through the veil of snow they appeared to be drifting like birds on a sea of mist.

Keeping away from the threatening pine branches along the shoulder of the road, I slid in short steps down its icy center, following the footprints left by the people ahead of me. Angelika clung to my arm. Her cheerfulness had evaporated.

"I'm scared," she said through her scarf.

"We're going home. That's all." I shrugged casually, but I did not feel confident. My muffled words went through my scarf in puffs of steam.

Angelika sniffled. "But I don't know the way."

I saw Miss Machulova ahead of me leaning into the snow.

"Follow Miss Machulova," I said and nudged her arm out of mine.

"I'll get lost if I don't hold on to you."

"Just stay close. I can't move with you hanging on to me."

We followed Miss Machulova's tracks in silence. Her barely visible outline drifted ahead of us. Snowflakes continued to float down.

The forest gave way to dormant fields. The smudged shapes of village houses appeared on the horizon like charcoal strokes. Black dots hurried from them toward the road. These villagers, their bodies wrapped like Egyptian mummies, joined the line of refugees. Hundreds trudged along the roads, littering them with discarded suitcases, cars that had run out of gasoline, bicycles with flat tires, and clothes that had become a burden to carry.

The extra clothes I had on hampered my movement. I stopped, removed my coat, took off the extra sweater, and discarded it on the side of the road. People moved past me like ghosts. While I had stopped to remove my sweater, I lost Angelika and Miss Machulova in the pulsating gray mass. The forest was behind me now, and an expanse of silent white fields spread to left and right. A muffled rolling sound broke the silence. The column of refugees parted and fled into the barren whiteness, scattering like field mice north and south.

The sound grew louder. Dark objects broke through the white wall and the roar of engines blasted the silence, drowning out the drumbeat of my own heart.

Soldiers on motorcycles with sidecars passed by, their rifles slung across their backs. Trucks and tanks loaded with armed men slid toward me on the frozen road. The roar of the engines shook the ground. A motorcyclist slipped on the icy road and tumbled into the ditch.

I ran into the field and followed the vanishing dark spots. A smudged shape loomed just ahead. I stopped dead. Through the noise of the tanks I heard a bare whisper of a sniffle.

"Angelika?" My voice was muffled by falling snow and by the rumble of trucks and tanks. I took a cautious step forward. Angelika had removed her frozen scarf from her mouth and was wiping her nose with her coat sleeve.

"You'll have icicles dropping from your nose," I said.

She gave me a sad smile.

We trudged through the fields hand in hand. The snow lay in deep drifts and we sank up to our knees. From time to time we stopped to let our pounding hearts rest.

We were alone in a silent whiteness broken by the distant sound of rolling trucks and tanks. We trudged and rested, trudged and rested. The cold penetrated the layers of clothing and numbed my body. My feet felt like blocks of ice.

The landscape did not change. The horizon kept slipping away, as if we had not moved. In the descending evening, the outline of a building floated into view on the sea of snow like a ghost ship. A pale glow came from a window. Energized by the welcoming yellow light, we plodded through the snow anticipating the warmth that surely awaited us.

I knocked on the door. Please, please let there be someone, I wailed silently. Behind us was the expanse of nothingness that could be rent at any moment by the rumble of tanks. The lace curtains parted. A round peasant face frowned into the darkness, then vanished. This time, I pounded on the window. A beam of light broke through the darkness and a welcoming warmth floated through the door as the woman opened it and stood undecided on the threshold. She watched us for a moment as we beat our arms across our chests and stamped our feet in the snow by her door.

Then she made her decision. "Get in," she said, and impatiently grabbed me by one arm and Angelika by the other to drag us into a warm room lit by an oil lamp.

Puddles formed on the worn wood floor as the snow melted from our coats.

"Take off your clothes." She disappeared behind a curtain and reappeared carrying two blankets.

Our clothes lay in wet piles on the floor. Without a word, she rubbed us down with a scratchy cloth, wrapped the blankets around us, and pushed us to the wood stove. She hung the wet clothes on a rope strung from wall to wall across the stove. The drips sizzled when they fell on the stove where a kettle of potato soup bubbled, filling the kitchen with an aroma of onions and bacon that made me drool.

The peasant woman, of stout proportions and a round, pink face, stood at the wooden table in the center of the room in her striped apron and smiled. Then she took a large round loaf of bread from the shelf above the stove, held it against her ribs, and cut thick, heavy slices toward herself with a sharp butcher knife. She spread goose grease on the slices of bread and salted them. Eager to get my teeth into a slice, I snatched the bread out of her hand and chewed so fast I choked. The grease eased the passage of the pungent bread.

Then she ladled some potato soup into bowls, set them before us, and urged us to eat. I blew on the soup and slurped the thick mush in greedy gulps. The woman's smile crinkled her round, pink cheeks.

She poured some coffee into two large earthen mugs and laced it with bubbling milk and sugar. The bittersweet liquid flowed into my body and warmed me down to my toes.

We slept curled under the kitchen table wrapped in the rough woolen blankets like hibernating animals. My sleep was intermittent, interrupted by roaring sounds of tanks and the hushed despair of people running for their lives. In the morning we slipped into our warm, dried clothes. The woman shoved two bowls of gruel topped with a thick slice of bread across the table.

Angelika, who was usually a complainer, had not said anything at all about the food or the sleeping arrangements. She seemed unusually composed.

The woman took some dough from the top of the stove, plunked it on the table she had covered with flour, and began to knead. We watched her large hands repeatedly press the dough against the table and turn it over.

"Which way is Prague?" I asked.

The woman pointed a flour-covered finger in the direction from which we had come, but did not look up from her kneading.

"We came from that road," I said. To go back to that road would be like walking into a trap.

Understanding the reluctance in my voice, she nodded and stopped kneading. "You can cut across the field and avoid the road."

She wiped her hands on her apron, sliced some more bread, and wrapped it in newspaper.

"I don't want to go back to that road," Angelika said with a mouthful of gruel.

"We'll cut across the field," I said, even though I did not know where the field would lead us.

We thanked the woman. She nodded her good-bye and watched us walk around the house into the white vastness. Angelika trudged behind me hiccuping.

"If you don't stop crying, you'll have frozen diamonds on your cheeks."

She wiped her face with the end of her scarf and kept sniveling.

The field was endless. The snow reached into nothingness, to the end of the earth. We walked for hours. Dusk began creeping over the land, hiding what few landmarks there were. I did not know where we were or how much longer we had to keep moving. Angelika was walking behind me like a silent ghost. I was afraid of what lay ahead. Was my mother all right? Was my father back from Bratislava? The fear of losing them pushed me to greater effort to move forward.

We came to a road and walked in the wagon ruts flanked by fields that stretched to the horizon. We slipped on the frozen ruts, but they made walking easier and faster. Even so, it seemed as if there would be nothing at the end of the road but a precipice.

A farmer stopped his cart, drawn by an emaciated horse. "Want a ride?"

"Are you going to Prague?"

"Kladno. You have to go through town to get there."

We climbed into the cart. It smelled of manure. He took us to town and offered us lodging. Again, we slept on the floor in the kitchen by the stove, and again our clothes hung overhead drip-drying, in the morning, fortified with gruel, bread, and warm clothes we were anxious to get going.

The farmer offered us a ride to the outskirts of Prague. The bouncing, ill-smelling ride seemed to go on forever. Then the road split into a hollow and a cluster of lights appeared in the distance.

"Look, Angelika. That must be Prague."

"Are you sure?"

"No, but what else could it be?"

The farmer stopped the cart and helped us out. He gave us directions to the streetcar terminal, patted us on the head, turned his cart around, and called out, "God be with you."

Though by now we were exhausted, we were energized by the thought of finally getting home. I urged Angelika on and we trudged through the snow, renewed by an urgent need for food and warmth.

The city was covered with snow. Soldiers were marching down the street. Panicked crowds scattered in all directions. German troops had occupied Prague while we were sleeping under the farmer's kitchen table. Already they had mounted loudspeakers on lampposts and trees. German flags hung from windows and lined the street. In patriotic defiance of the invaders, a solitary Czech flag hung limply atop a lightning rod. A streetcar full of people stood at the terminal. More people hung from its doors and windows and clung tenuously to the roof. The snow in the street was trampled into ice as more people slipped and slid across the street to reach the streetcar. Those fortunate enough to have a hold kicked away those who tried to get on. Angelika held on to my coat belt as I tried to push my way through the crowd. As I was forced off the platform, I felt my belt rip from my coat. I turned to take Angelika's hand, but the waves of people pushed her farther away from me till she vanished from my view.

I yelled for her, but the sound was lost in the clanking of the streetcar and the shouted announcements.

"Achtung! Achtung!" The loudspeakers blared across the tumult of the crowd, but the rest of the announcement was lost in the confused shouts and screams of people being left behind by the screeching wheels of the streetcar as it moved away.

I walked up and down the street calling Angelika, but she had disappeared. She probably was on her way home, I thought.

I pushed through the crowd on the platform and crossed to the sidewalk. Tanks rolled down the center of the street and bit tread patterns into the cobblestones. The distant tattoo of drums floated through the dusk like a dirge.

People rushed past me and disappeared around corners. Soon the street was deserted.

Streetlamps formed pools of light on the frozen snow. A woman rushed past me, then stopped suddenly and turned back to me.

"Curfew," she said and grabbed my coat sleeve. "Didn't you hear the announcement?"

Searching for Angelika amid the rattle of the tanks I had not paid attention to the announcer.

"No," I said, and pulled away from her.

"You've got to get off the street," she said.

"What for? I'm going home." I walked away.

"Don't you understand? They shoot on sight," she said to my back.

I turned to face her. "I've got to get home." I was terrified that if I did not get home right then when I was so close, I might not see my parents again.

"Come on. You can go home tomorrow," she whispered and looked furtively around.

The urgency in her voice spoke of danger that unnerved me. Reluctantly, I fell into a trot beside her. We stopped at a house in an alley. The woman looked from side to side, then quickly unlocked the door and pulled me inside. A dim orange bulb lit the stairwell. The banister cast eerie shadows against the wall.

I followed her up the stairs, feeling my way along the wall. She stopped on the third floor, listened, then unlocked the door to the right and waved me into a large room. She turned on the solitary bulb dangling from the ceiling, it hung over a round table littered with books. Next to the books were a full ashtray, a loaf of bread on a plate, and two dirty cups. Two hooks screwed into the wall held pieces of clothing piled one on top of another. A tile stove in the window corner radiated warmth. A tin bucket filled with coal stood to the side. A rumpled bed was pushed against the wall under the window.

"Close the door."

"I have to get home." Tears choked me into silence.

"I can't let you go out there," she said with an impatient gesture. She pulled me inside and closed the door.

"But you don't understand—" My words turned into hiccups.

She put her arms around my shoulder and led me to a chair. "Rest a while, anyway."

A sharp pang of fear suffocated me and tears pooled behind my lids.

"Everything'll be all right," she said.

She removed my coat and hung it over the sink in the bath-kitchen. A piece of plywood covered the tub and served as a kitchen counter on which stood a Primus cooker. Next to it was a sink. Two pots hung on hooks over the sink. The base of the sink was curtained and hid a few dishes. In the opposite corner was the toilet.

She lit the cooker, filled a pot with water, and placed it on the flame. When the water boiled, she removed the pot and threw in a handful of ground coffee retrieved from behind the curtain under the sink. The coffee rose in foamy slush.

"You can slice the bread."

I pushed a pile of books aside and sliced the hardened bread into thick, uneven slices. The woman rinsed out the dirty cups, brought two chipped plates from under the sink, and poured the foamy brew through a sieve into the two stained cups. As I sipped the strong, black coffee that smelled of Mother's kitchen, visions of black uniforms leading my mother off into a covered truck closed my throat. I jumped up and grabbed my coat.

"What's the matter?"

"I have to get home. Mother will worry."

She looked at me, her dark eyes misty.

"Eat." Her head tilted as she watched me put on my coat. "I suspect your mother would rather worry than mourn." She roughly removed my coat and threw it on the rumpled bed.

"You haven't a chance out there." She pushed me back into the chair, sat down across from me, and lit a cigarette.

After some silence, she said, "I'm Minna."

She was a woman of indeterminate age. Short, slim, and energetic in her movements, she gave the impression of youth, yet her sad, dark eyes were framed by wrinkles and veiled an underlying sadness.

"I'm Miriam."

She gave me a quick smile.

I picked up the bread and continued to nibble on it, while Minna convinced me to spend the night.

The floor was cold and hard. In spite of using Minna's fur-lined coat as a blanket, I shivered. Minna sat on her rumpled bed, her feet tucked under her like a tailor. Her profile was outlined by the faint yellow glint of a streetlamp. The red hypnotic glow of her cigarette traveled in an arc to her mouth, brightened as she inhaled and then dimmed.

I fell into a fitful sleep.

The clatter of the coal shovel awakened me. Stars of frost clung to the still dark window. I slipped on my dress and wool knit stockings, splashed my face with water from the sink, and sat down at the table. Minna poured coffee and we shared the leftover bread.

Large, translucent flakes began to fall as she walked me to the streetcar stop. The train clanked around a curve and came to a screeching halt. Bodies were crushed inside, and as the door opened some fell out. Minna shoved me through the cursing crowd onto the doorstep where I clung to the handrail, impeding the closing of the door.

"Get off the step," the conductor yelled through the mass of bodies.

I couldn't move. Someone pulled me up by my coat collar and several hands pushed others off the steps. As the door closed, I was pressed against its glass. The people left on the platform shook their fists and cursed as the streetcar screeched toward the city's center along its frozen tracks.

I watched Minna's forlorn figure through the hazy window till she disappeared from sight. I did not know her last name.

I alighted at Vaclavske namesti. Tanks lined the street and soldiers filled the sidewalk. Hurriedly I crossed the street and turned into Spanelska Street. It was a short walk to number six.

The apartment door had never been locked, but it was now. I pounded my fists against its heavy wood. At last I heard the bolt unlock. Mother's tear-stained face greeted me.

"Come in quickly." She pulled me inside.

Nora was with her. Father's manuscripts were scattered on the hearth. Flames licked the chimney.

"What's happening?" I asked, watching sheets of paper flying up the flue.

"School closed three days ago. Where have you been?"

Where had I been? I had no idea it had been three days since I had left school. The sequence of events was a disorganized jumble I could not explain. I remained silent. She took me into her arms. Tears dropped onto my head.

"You're wet through," she said and gently pulled off my coat and pushed me to the fire. She sat beside me shredding Father's manuscripts and throwing them into the fire. Nora kept handing her sheaves of paper. Flames shot out of the open stove each time Mother threw in a handful of torn pages. Her shoulders heaved and her hands shook as she shredded the papers.

"Why are you destroying Father's manuscripts?"

"You know why. They are anti-Nazi articles."

I knew that. It was why we had left Germany in such a hurry. I watched her destroy my father's work with growing anxiety.

"Where is Father?" I asked at last.

She stopped shredding the paper but did not turn around. Nora began to cry.

I sensed something terrible had happened, but I did not want to know it. I walked into the kitchen, hoping that it would go away.

"They arrested him yesterday," my mother said as I was almost through the door. I could not move. The fear that had followed me through the snowy fields materialized now in the air like a solid block of ice. I was numb. My voice froze, I could not even cry. Then I walked to my mother. She was mechanically throwing Father's condemnation of the Nazis into the fire. I grabbed her hand to stop her. "This is Father's work. If you destroy it we will have nothing left of him."

"If I don't, we'll all die." Resolutely she pushed me away from her and kept feeding the stove.

Arrested. I knew that people were arrested and disappeared in Germany. Some were tortured, some shot. Not here. Not my father. Not the man who taught me to read and write before I went to school. Not the man who sometimes took me on assignments, the man who gave the family stability and a sense of security and made me feel beautiful and intelligent.

I watched my mother's soundless weeping. My own pain was beyond tears. I was filled with anguished rage at those who had caused me pain so tangible I could touch it.

"Maybe they'll release him. They released Lex," I said without conviction.

"They no longer release prisoners. There is no hope of that."

That night I did not sleep, torn between hope and despair. I did not understand the why of it. What had we done to elicit such hatred? How could strangers come into your home and drag you away without reason? Why were we so helpless? Was it because we had no guns? What gave people power over others? I thought and thought but found no answer.

The next morning at breakfast, I was so exhausted from the three-day trudge to Prague and the fear of losing my father to possible torture and death that I fell asleep in my chair.

Mother woke me gently. My first thought: "Is Father back?"

"No, dear."

I had forgotten about Angelika. The thought of her having been taken chilled me through and through and I broke out into a sweat.

"I must see if Angelika is home." I rushed across the landing. No one was home. Had they been taken too? I was so upset, I could not even cry. My mother called across the landing for me to come along. She looked drawn and listless and her eyes were dull. I stood momentarily immobile by Angelika's door, and then slid to the floor crying great wracking sobs. My mother tried to console me but I could not stop.

"We have to meet Lex and Steffie," she said as she tried to pull me off the floor. Her voice was flat. I did not care. Kurt's mangled body bounced around in my head like a spirit trying to get out from its confinement, and then he became Angelika, and then my father. I could not see these three figures as they had been once, full of life and laughter. I thought I was going mad. The world was collapsing around me.

"Angelika will be all right, you'll see," Mother said, but I heard her as if through a veil of water. She took me under my shoulders and pulled me up. We stood huddled together for a long time. My despair was so deep that I felt I was drowning in it. Slowly, slowly I stopped crying. I held on to my mother's comforting warmth, but I knew then that neither her warmth nor my tears would alter anything.

"We're going to be late," Mother said. I put on my coat, wrapped my scarf across my mouth, and tripped along behind Mother with Nora in tow.

The city was devoid of Czech sounds. The guttural sounds of bellowed commands, the march of solid boots, and the rat-tat-tat of drums floated through the air along the boulevard. Troops swarmed through the city, trampling down the snow. Patrols scoured the streets. Paralyzing fear spread through the city, shuttering windows and doors. I tried not to be afraid and pretended I did not see the patrols.

We crossed the marketplace. The vegetable stands were tightly wrapped with tarpaulin. A few peasants stood around silently, their arms folded across their chests, watching soldiers at the other end of the marketplace toppling the statue of Masaryk. My head was tightly tucked into my coat collar in the hope that perhaps I would not be seen. Mother tightened her hold on my hand and pulled me along. We took the long way around to the Café Kotva. We walked as fast as we could, trying not to cause suspicion. Several times we ducked into doorways to avoid the armed patrol.

My heart beat faster when I saw Chris walking on the sidewalk across the street with his father. I was about to call to him when my mother squeezed my hand so tightly it hurt. I had been told that I must not recognize anyone, lest I implicate them or they us. When I saw Chris I forgot the admonition. Our eyes met and held for a moment as he walked past. I tagged along beside my mother, my heart splintering into a thousand shards.

We fought our way through the crowd jamming the cul-de-sac. The Kotva was crowded, with standing room only. Zelezny pushed people away from the table he always saved for us. He was nervous and apprehensive.

I moved the curtains aside and watched hundreds of fists hammer against the shut doors of the embassies on the street. The mass of bodies pulsed with panic and flowed in circles. Voices rose in a rush of shrillness demanding that the doors be opened. The doors remained shut.

The Café Kotva was filled with whispered reassurances.

I sat on the recessed windowsill scanning the crowd for some sign of Lex and Steffie. Then I saw their heads bobbing in the mass of swirling bodies, trying to push their way through. Lex waved toward the Café's window. I waved back.

Zelezny jostled his way through the knots of people, carrying two cups of coffee that spilled into the saucers. He placed them on the table and wiped the saucers with his apron. He shrugged apologetically. His round, rosy face drooped. Even his belly seemed to sag.

"You look tired," he said.

"János was arrested," Mother said. I had never heard her voice sound so dead.

Zelezny took a step back and clutched his chest, then walked away wiping his eyes with his apron.

"Look, there's Lex," I said.

Mother turned to look just as Lex disappeared in the crowd. He kept popping up like a swimmer overcoming waves.

Zelezny returned and put his hands on Mother's shoulders. "I wish they'd let him through," he said, his dark, arched eyebrows wrinkling his forehead. Mother was rummaging in her purse for some coins.

Suddenly the shouting stopped and heads turned to the entrance of the street. Trucks were backing into the cul-de-sac and forcing people against the buildings, closing off the street. Flanked by SS officers in their black and silver, soldiers jumped out of the trucks, rifles at the ready. Shrill voices rose against the Café's window as women, children, and men were herded toward the trucks. Steffie was among them. Lex stretched his arm across the bobbing heads in a vain attempt to reach Steffie's hand. She was pushed farther and farther away from him and finally forced by rifle butts into a truck. Her hands clung to the tailgate as it slammed shut. The packed truck drove away and another backed into the street. More people were rounded up. The ones left behind forced themselves into the Café in an attempt to get away, and Lex was pushed against the far wall.

"Let me out," he shouted, but the shoving and shouting mass of people imprisoned him. The second truck pulled out as soon as it was filled. A tense silence filled the room, as palpable as smoke. It rose against the windowpane like an invisible reproach. Shrill voices lingered, engraved into the stillness.

I wanted to run out there and save Steffie, but my limbs seemed to have turned to water.

Then the panicked customers crowded through the door and vanished. I felt my blood rush into my ears. Mother stood motionless, staring into the empty street, her arms reaching into space. Zelezny stared at the coins Mother had placed in his outstretched hand. He took Mother's hand, pressed the coins into it, and quickly walked away.

Her eyes glazed, Mother said, "Miriam?"

Reassured that I was there, Mother patted me on the head. She stood by the window and stared into the empty street, her hands cupping her temples. My knees weakened at the sound of Mother's weeping.

I tried to console her, but sobs choked my words.

My lovely Steffie was gone. I could still see her reaching for Lex, terror distorting her beautiful face.

Lex' face was white. His hands reached into the void, his broken fingers curled like wilting flowers, his body motionless.

Zelezny came with two glasses of cognac. He placed them on the table with shaking hands. He took Mother by the shoulder and pushed her into the chair.

"Drink it. It'll make you feel better."

Zelezny held the glass to her mouth and tipped it. The cognac ran down her chin. She began to cough. Zelezny patted her on the back, then poured more cognac in her mouth. She seemed to awaken from a trance.

Then Zelezny put his arm around Lex's shoulder and walked him to the table. He handed him the cognac. "Drink!"

Lex threw the liquid down in a gulp and sat down opposite Mother.

"I'll get you some soup," Zelezny said to me, and left.

I sat across from Mother and Lex, my hands tight in my lap. I was unable to comprehend what had just happened. It was not real. I must have dreamed it. But there was Lex, his tall lean body hunched over the table and Mother crying on his shoulder.

It started to snow again. Soft flakes fell to the ground, covering the hollow footprints and the truck tracks. The doors to the embassies remained shut. The day faded quickly. The Café remained empty except for an occasional patron who wandered into the Kotva, sat for a while, then left.

Zelezny reappeared with two bowls of soup and put down one for me and one for Nora. "Come on, eat! It'll make you feel better."

I sipped the soup. The warm, delicious liquid eased the somersaults in my stomach. Suddenly Mother rose and grabbed me by the arm. The spoon fell out of my hand and clattered to the floor.

"We have to leave." Her voice was urgent.

Zelezny jumped up and took her arm off mine. "It's curfew. You can spend the night in my apartment downstairs."

Lex pulled Mother into the chair. Zelezny picked up the spoon, wiped it in his apron, and handed it to me.

"I have to get home before curfew," Mother said.

"Curfew is on. Come downstairs," Zelezny said.

Reluctantly, Mother let Zelezny lead her. Lex took Nora and me by the hand and led us downstairs.

We spent the night in Zelezny's sitting room. Nora and I slept on the sofa, Mother and Lex on the floor. The following morning Lex walked home with us through a fresh layer of snow. He made a fire and we sat around it in silence. My thoughts were drumming in my head. I was sad, angry, and sick, but I would not give in to the tears that pooled behind my eyes.

"You're going to have to get the girls out of here," Lex said, throwing more wood into the stove.

His words rolled around my head, their weight oppressing me with the memory of our last border crossing. I felt as though the veins inside my body were collapsing and my bones crumbling into a pile of ashes. My heart beat in rhythm with the wind drumming against the window.

Beskyd Mountains

While Lex played checkers with Nora, Mother wrapped two slices of bread and a hunk of cheese and stuffed it into my left coat pocket. She pinned a ticket to Frydek—a town in the Beskyd Mountains by the Polish border—to the inside of my coat, tore a sheet from her notebook, and scribbled something on it.

"Here's your Uncle Charles's address in New York."

I put it into my right coat pocket.

"Write to me as soon as you get to England. And write to Uncle Charles."

"I want to stay with you. Please let me stay."

"We'll meet in England," Mother said. I heard the catch in her throat.

"Why can't you go with me?"

"This is organized by the Underground for children only."

"What is that?"

"They're friends to people in need."

"Do I know them?"

"You'll know them as your friends throughout your journey."

"But I don't want to go."

"You can't stay here." She wiped my tears.

"Why isn't Nora going?"

"She's younger and will be going a different route from yours."

"Is she going to England, too?"

"Yes, she'll be there."

"How am I going to England?"

"First you'll go to Frydek."

"How?"

"By train. Someone there will guide you across the border into Poland."

She put on her coat and tied a scarf around her head.

"When will you come?"

"When I have my papers. At least you'll be safe."

"I don't want to be safe. I want to stay with you."

"Think of it as a great adventure." Her voice did not sound convincing. I clung to her.

"You're a sensible twelve-year-old girl. It's more important than ever to be sensible. And remember, with common sense one can live anywhere." I did not want to be sensible. I did not want to live anywhere else. I wanted to be here, with my family, my friends, the things I knew and understood.

She stroked my head and patted my cheek. "Now, wipe your tears and smile."

I could not bring myself to smile, not even to please her.

"I'll be in England within a month. That's not so long, is it?"

What if a month was never? An icy chill raced through my veins. A reel of slow-moving scenes floated on an orchestra of cries all around me.

"What if you can't come?"

"I'll come," she said. "Come now, smile." She stroked my chin to coax my mouth into a smile. But it was paralyzed. I felt entombed in an ice coffin. Fear had petrified my heart and turned my body rigid.

She took the family portrait from her desk and removed it from its frame and handed it to me. It had a crack now that curved from Mother's shoulder to her breast and one that ran down between my father and me as if to separate us.

In the portrait, Father sits with his left hand firmly planted on his thigh. His artist's cravat is bursting from a white shirt collar and a pen is protruding from the pocket of his dark suit. His finely chiseled, delicate features are unbroken by a smile, and his dark eyes are focused on some distant object. Next to him sits Mother, her thin, solemn face expressing restraint and sadness. On her lap is dark-haired, dark-eyed, one-year-old Nora. Front and center, I am sitting on a rocking horse holding on to its mane, a round-faced, brown-eyed three-year-old towhead smiling mysteriously, as if I alone had escaped the somber aspects of life. My mother's hair is in a long braid, but my hair is cropped short like a boy's, its whiteness conspicuous even in this black-and-white photo.

The portrait floated before my brimming eyes and dissolved into a wash of gray.

"Come on, Miriam, roll it up."

I could not move. She took it out of my hand and rolled it as she had done in Berlin, but this time she slid a rubber band around it. I put it in the pocket with Uncle Charles's address.

"There. Now we can go," she said.

I hugged Nora and Lex, feeling it was good-bye forever.

Mother took me by the hand and we walked down the stairs. I looked back to wave one last good-bye to Lex, who was standing in the door holding Nora.

We hurried to the Wilson railroad station. We dared not run lest we arouse suspicion. The houses on both sides of the cobbled street tilted threateningly toward me, and the red flags with black swastikas in white circles waved dangerously from windows and lampposts. A Nazi flag had even been placed in the hand of St. Wenceslaus sitting on his horse in front of the National Gallery. The trees lining Wenceslaus Square were bare and the street glistened with new snow. Snow covered the branches of the barren trees. The cobblestones were slick with trampled snow and we slid along like skaters. The sound of boots slapping the icy cobblestones seemed to pursue us. The sidewalks were crowded with mournful faces watching men in shiny black boots and smoothly pressed uniforms marching in columns of eight and carrying banners down the wide boulevard. Boys in short brown pants and brown leather belts marched to the rat-tat-tat of the drummers.

Otto was marching in the front row, beating a drum. Now proud and pressed, with his chin up, he still looked to me to be a worm. I choked at the thought of being forced to run because of this pitiable piece of Hitler Youth whom I could have easily beaten up. Still, the hollow sound of the drums and the solid slap of marching boots made me uneasy. I clung to Mother's hand.

The marching feet paraded toward us. On the outside of a column, all in black with silver trim, the visor of his black cap bearing the skull-and-crossbones insignia, marched Obermeier. I stopped and gave him what I thought to be a contemptuous look. Our eyes met briefly, but there was no flicker of recognition in his.

"Don't stop," Mother said, and dragged me into a side street.

She glanced back and quickened her pace. I tripped along behind her as we fled through narrow alleys. My breath came in spurts.

A solid wall of people blocked the entrance to the railroad station. Elbows extended, Mother forced her way through the mass of people inch by inch. Screams and whistles rose above the hiss of the steam engine. The shouts of the conductor were muffled by the surge of pressing bodies. The mass of bodies crushed the air out of me. Mother pushed me through a cluster of people hanging from the train doors and forced me into the corridor. Some unknown hands hoisted me into the luggage net. Through the top of the window I saw my mother's head disappear in the crush of the milling crowd. I waved frantically through the open window. If only she would turn to wave. "Mother!" My cry was lost in the tumult. Oh, please dear God, let her not be lost to me, I prayed. I sensed this was my last good-bye to her and feared I would always have to remember her being swallowed by the crowd, disappearing as if she never had been there on the platform with me. Now I was alone, not sure where I was going or if I would get there.

A hiss of steam, and a whistle, and the train lurched forward. My feet dangled from the luggage netting over anonymous heads. My view was limited to the ceiling and the sign over of the red emergency brakes. "Pull handle in case of emergency," I read over and over.

The train crept along, stopping at every village and junction but unable to take on more passengers.

Toward the end of the day I had to go to the lavatory. I managed to get someone's attention and was hoisted down. Imitating my mother, I forced my way through the corridor to the lavatory with my elbows. After an interminable wait I was at last able to get in. Unable to get back to my luggage rack, I remained pressed in the corner between the exit and the lavatory door, which banged me repeatedly as people entered and exited the toilet. Sometime before dark I managed to eat the bread and cheese my mother had stuffed into my coat pocket.

The following day we arrived in Olomouc. Unable to resist the force of bodies, I was pushed, turned, tugged, and propelled through the station and into the street. Battered and disoriented, my legs infirm, I pressed myself against a wall and waited till the station was deserted, then walked to the stationmaster's office and knocked on the door.

A man opened the door and looked down at me. He had on a blue uniform and blue cap with the Slovak emblem. Unlike the spit-and-polish of the Nazi uniforms I had become used to, his was crumpled and stained. His black mustache almost reached his ears.

"Yes?"

I could think only of water and sleep. "May I have some water?"

He looked around the empty station. "You alone?"

"Yes. May I have some water?"

"Come on in."

The windows were steamed from the water simmering in a kettle on the woodstove.

"Here." He handed me a bottle of wine and a piece of sausage and smiled with the corners of his mouth.

I gulped some wine, chewed on the sausage, and drank more wine. The stationmaster stood with one hand on his hip, and the other stroking his mustache. He watched the wine drip down my chin. I fell asleep in the chair and drifted through banks of snow pursued by Obermeier.

"Wake up."

The strange man standing over me startled me. My head felt sluggish and my lids heavy.

"I'm going off duty now," said the stationmaster.

He waited for me to say something. I wasn't sure what he had said. His frame swayed before my eyes. I could still taste the wine.

"Where are you going?" he said.

I sat up and struggled with the pin Mother had used to attach the ticket to the inside of my coat. He watched, twirling his mustache with his thumb and index finger. I handed him the ticket.

"Frydek? You missed the train."

"I think I'm supposed to be there today," I said without eagerness or conviction. I wanted to sleep.

"You'll have to wait till tomorrow."

I was bewildered and frightened. Where was I going? What was I doing here? I looked out the window. The snow was shoulder-deep.

"Can I stay here?"

"Come along." He waved his arm toward the door.

I staggered behind him out into the night. The snow sparkled in the shafts of light streaming from windows. My ears burned from the cold and my nose dripped. We stopped at a house from whose windows the glow of light danced in the snow. The smell of freshly baked bread greeted me when he opened the door. A round, cheerful woman was slicing a loaf of bread, placing the slices on the kitchen table. The stationmaster removed his hat and coat.

"Take off your coat," the woman said, and continued to slice the bread.

The stationmaster nudged me onto a wooden bench, and with his tight smile pushed a slice of bread under my nose.

The woman ladled milk out of a barrel into an earthen mug and handed it to me. Her eyes were friendly as she watched me gulp the milk.

I slept in the kitchen warmed by the stove and a feather bed, with the stationmaster's dog as my companion.

The next morning the woman gave me two slices of bread wrapped in newspaper and some diluted wine she poured into a jam jar. The stationmaster walked me back to the station. He explained that I had to take a train to Prerov and there change to another train for Frydek, and he gave me detailed instructions on platform, time, and direction. None of it had sounded so complicated when my mother had explained it.

The train rolled in and stopped. I climbed on, sorry to say good-bye to the kind stationmaster. The stationmaster blew his whistle, swung his wooden paddle, and the train chugged out. I leaned out of the window and waved. The stationmaster tipped his hat.

The empty wooden benches, polished by years of wear, ran the length of both sides of the car. The train crept through snow-covered fields and wound through forests. As it climbed higher into the mountains, it became colder. I had no idea where I was going nor where all these places were that I was supposed to get to. Falling snow melted against the window. The country rolled by and looked as desolate as I felt. I wanted to go home.

I alighted in Prerov, walked down the deserted platform, and crossed the railroad tracks as I had been instructed to do by the stationmaster in Olomouc.

A swig of the diluted wine sent a warm glow to my cheeks.

Ahead loomed the Beskyd Mountains with their tiers of snow covered forests. An engine laboring up the mountain and belching steam came around the bend. The locomotive was pulling only a caboose. The conductor leaned out and scanned the platform.

"Frydek?" I shouted over the steam.

"Yep." He gave me his hand and pulled me up the steep step into the caboose. He indicated a seat by a window opposite a peasant woman. On the floor beside her was a cage with a goose jutting its neck through the grating.

The conductor blew his whistle and waved his paddle. The engine coughed and its wheels began to turn.

I watched the goose strain through the bars of the cage. The woman forced its head back in. As soon as she had done so, the goose squeezed through the bars again.

The engine coughed its way up the forested mountains. The boughs of the pines were bent under the weight of the snow and snapped back as the snow slid off the laden branches. A mist enveloped the peaks of the Beskydy. In the slow, laborious climb of the train, images superimposed themselves one upon another. Panicked cities merged into silent country, deserted platforms melted into crowded streets.

The woman, her babushka firmly tied around her head, stared at me.

"Stranger," she said, pointing at me.

Confused, I shifted in my seat and looked out the window.

"Ej! You don't talk?"

I turned away from the window and watched the goose struggle in its confined space. I thought of the luggage rack I had been confined to and felt sympathy for the goose.

"Ej! Cat got your tongue?"

Unable to formulate a coherent reply, I pointed at the goose. "Your goose wants out."

The woman's belly wobbled. "Hee, hee, hee," laughter exploded from her heaving bosom. The goose's head bounced against the cage.

"Did, did, did you hear that?" she stuttered to the conductor.

"You'd want out too if you were in there." The conductor slapped his thighs with both hands.

Startled by the hilarity I had provoked, I turned to the window again while the conductor and the woman bantered.

At Strasnice, the conductor helped the woman down. The goose nipped her in the nose as she struggled down the steps, with both arms wrapped around the cage. She waddled down the deserted platform cursing.

The conductor and I continued the journey in silence. At Frydek he helped me get off. Night had dropped its black curtain and the only visible light came from the stationmaster's hut. I walked over and knocked. The door opened and yet another stationmaster looked me over and yawned.

"Can I come in?" I said.

"Sure, sure. Hurry. The cold is blowing in." He quickly closed the door and directed me to the stove.

"Warm yourself." He pushed me to the stove.

We stood at the stove rubbing our hands together and stomping our feet. Soft smoke curled from a pipe stuck between his teeth.

"Do you know where Milos the shepherd lives?" I said. In these mountain villages everyone knew everyone, so Mother had said. He nodded and blew smoke through his nostrils. "Lives up the mountain." He indicated the direction with his pipe and scratched his head under his cap.

I knew not to tell him that Milos was to get me across the border.

He took three quick puffs of his pipe and blew the smoke at the frosted window. The smoke curled against it and dissipated at the ceiling. "Can't get up that mountain path at night."

"I have to," I said. I was a day late already. If I stayed, I would be two days late.

He looked into the darkness toward the mountain. "You can't. You can sleep behind the stove on the bench."

The bench did not look comfortable, but I was too tired to care.

"I'll take you to the path in the morning." He was talking to the window. Before I could say anything, he was through the door. I slept in my coat, curled like a cat behind the stove.

He came in the morning with a mug of coffee and a loaf of bread and watched me eat and drink while he puffed on his pipe and filled the hut with a fragrant haze.

Later we plodded silently through the snow up the sloping village street. The dozen or so small houses, with snow piled on their windowsills, crouched under their white burden like hibernating mice. The street narrowed into a barely visible path that disappeared into the forest. The stationmaster stopped and pointed into the forest.

"Milos's hut is a ways up. To the right is the border guard's hut. Just stay on the path and you'll avoid him."

"A guard?" I said. No one had said anything about a guard.

"Just stay on the path," he said.

Firs and pines brushed against each other and seemed impenetrable. I turned to ask where the path was but he was gone.

A narrow depression flanked by drifts of snow was barely visible under the laden branches. It wound steeply around trees and disappeared into the still, dark forest. From time to time a snapping branch broke the silence as the snow dropped with a thud. My breath floated ahead of me in puffs of steam as I labored through deep drifts using trees as markers of my progress. Occasionally I stopped to catch my breath. Low gusts of wind spun the snow and whirled it over my footprints, leaving no trace of my having been there. Cold grabbed me with its frosty fingers and penetrated through my clothes to my bones.

The mountain was watching. The woods were full of eyes. Tree branches reached out to me like clawing fingers. Each crack of a twig sounded like a shot. The guard could be right behind me. Shadows crept across my path as if to stop me. Shafts of light penetrated through the trees and glinted off patches of snow, making them shine like bright, hungry eyes watching me, ready to devour me.

The air grew steadily more oppressive and the darkness pressed against me. I heard a plopping sound behind me and turned. A sudden nightmarish conviction seized me: Obermeier was the guard and he'd discovered me. I wanted to burrow deep into the snow to hide from those watching eyes. I forced myself to go on. Then a smell of burning wood drifted through the trees and a glint of light skipped across the snow in strokes of yellow. A hut crouched in the snow at the end of the path. I quickened my steps and knocked on the door.

A large shadow fell across the path as the door opened.

"Milos?" I whispered.

He nodded, puffed once on his long-stemmed pipe, and stepped aside to let me enter. A round, carved table stood in the center of the room. Flowers painted in spirals wound around its legs. Two carved wooden chairs painted with the same design, a cot under the window, and a stove in a corner filled the room.

Milos helped me take off my coat and hung it on a chair. The melting snow dripped onto the worn, wooden floor. He ladled something out of a barrel with a wooden scoop and handed the scoop to me. White lumps of a spongy mass floated on an opaque liquid.

"What is it?"

"Clabbered milk."

I sucked the sour, pudding-like sponge from the wooden scoop with puckered lips. He stoked the fire, then sat down and rested his elbows on the table, his pipe tightly clamped between his teeth. "We'll climb to the top tomorrow. Vlada will take you down the other side into Poland," he said.

I accepted that statement the way I accepted the snow. It was there. Time did not matter anymore. Tomorrow, today, and yesterday blended into one long, dreary journey in which I was the unwilling traveler whose destination was unknown.

Milos knocked his pipe against the stove. The ashes dropped onto the floor. He stepped on them and put the pipe in his jacket pocket and offered me his cot covered with a soft feather bed. I fell into it and slept cradled in its warmth, more comfortable than I had been for a while. Milos slept on the floor.

After a breakfast of bread and clabbered milk, Milos tied my coat together with a piece of rope. "Keeps you warmer."

He put on his sheepskin coat, slung a scarf around his neck, and pulled a cap over his ears. He put cheese and bread into a rucksack and picked up a leather flask of wine. "Let's go," he said.

The climb was slow. We rested at the summit under a tree and ate cheese and bread. In the valley below to the south lay the Czech village from which I had come. Its houses jutted through the snow in small gray mounds. To the west, cut off from the village by deep forests, was a lake. Blackened by shadows, it lay in a hollow of the mountains like a dark eye. To the north, a steep mountain path wound through the trees into Poland.

Milos rose, brushed the snow off my coat, wrapped the scarf around his neck, and waved his hand in the direction of the path. He trod the path like a mountain goat. My steps left small impressions behind his large footprints. Eerie shadows crawled across the path as evening came and darkness dropped through the trees. Milos's blurred shape glided ahead of me like a phantom. Black branches whipped my face. The crunch of his footsteps was lost in the eerie silence, disorienting me completely and compelling me to stop. I had lost sight of Milos.

"Milos?" I whispered into the dark forest with chattering teeth, but there was no answer.

A shadow slid across the path. Steps crunched toward me in the snow. I dared not move. Then the shadow took shape and Milos appeared in silhouette. He stooped and tied his scarf around the rope holding my coat together, and wound the other end around his wrist. Led by the tug of the scarf, I stumbled behind him through the snow.

"We're almost there," he said.

A glimmer of light fluttered through the trees. An oil lamp in a window made a halo of light. A shaft of light poured onto the snow as the door to the hut opened, and Vlada welcomed Milos. They exchanged loud greetings, while I stood in the glow stomping my feet. After we entered, Milos dropped his sack and slapped Vlada on the back. They laughed and embraced. Puddles formed around my feet and steam rose from my clothes as I stood by the stove and watched the two men. Vlada, the Polish shepherd and owner of the hut, stroked his chin and looked me over. He turned to Milos.

"Hey, what a little thing."

"Sure is."

Milos slapped his thigh and laughed. They danced around the table, their arms held high above their heads.

I fell asleep on the cot. When I awoke, Milos was gone. Pale sunlight curled against the window and filtered into the room. Vlada fixed mush on the stove, then filled a small suitcase with food and clothing. We talked, he in Polish, I in Czech, and with gestures and some words similar in both languages we managed to understand each other.

After breakfast he cleaned the dishes in a pan filled with melted snow. When he had done the dishes, we dressed. He carried the suitcase outside and closed the door. We stepped into a large white expanse surrounded by forest. The hut was in the center of this plateau, guarded by a circle of trees. The vast white plateau could have cracked Icarus's wings with its brittle cold. Its crisp chill penetrated my coat as I walked across to the protection of the forest.

Vlada's footsteps crunched down the soft snow ahead of me. The path through the forest was now downhill and wound through head-high snow drifts that had gathered at the base of the trees. Where the path was steep and straight, we sat on the suitcase and used it as a sled. Vlada guided it with his feet and whooshed downhill like an expert tobogganer. Thrilled with the excitement of such speed, I held onto his waist and shouted, "Faster, faster."

Snow shot from under his feet into my face and forced me to close my eyes and mouth. Soon we had to abandon the ride and begin plodding through drifts of snow. Then the forest receded and the mountain slipped into a village. Two church steeples punctured the overcast sky. A horse-drawn cart waited on the road below. The horse pawed the mud and steam rose from its nostrils. A man leaned against the large wooden wheel of the cart, smoke from his pipe drifting in soft clouds toward the town. The men shook hands.

"Jerszy is taking you to Katowice for the train to Gdynia," Vlada said. He took my mitten-clad hand into his. "Good luck."

I watched him walk back up the slope. Halfway up he turned and waved, then disappeared into the trees. The warmth and comfort of Vlada's easygoing nature had thawed my apprehensions. Vlada was yet another person whose brief passage through my life left me feeling sad. But I had no time for sentiment.

Jerszy lifted me into the wagon, climbed in after me, and whipped the blinkered horse. The horse's head bounced up and down as it hauled us through mud ruts left by melting snow. Numb, I sat beside Jerszy as the horse labored downhill.

The behemoth railway station at Katowice lay at the foot of the hill. People were streaming in from all directions and disappearing under the dome. Steam belched against the glass ceiling and curled under it in a gray veil.

Jerszy tied up the horse in an alley behind the station. He lit his pipe and the flame of the match dropped down and flared up as he sucked at his pipe. He blew out the match and took a deep breath.

"The Germans have occupied Danzig. Whatever happens in there, don't say anything unless you can do it in German. Can you?"

I looked past him into the valley and nodded.

We walked down the slushy slope.

"In Gdynia, the code word at the wharf is 'Czezin.' A fisherman will be there every day at fourteen-hundred hours."

"What's that?"

"Two o'clock in the afternoon."

"I have no watch."

"You'll have to ask," he said.

Inside the station it was bedlam. All of Europe seemed to have been concentrated in railway stations. Jostled and buffeted by people trying to cram their way to the front of the line, Jerszy hoisted me on his shoulders and bulldozed through the crowd. At the ticket office he kept everyone at bay with his elbows. When he finally had the ticket in his hand, he hid it in the inside pocket of his overcoat, then jogged back into the alley behind the station. He lifted me down, looked right and left, then pulled the ticket from his coat and pinned it inside my coat

"Don't lose it."

Shortly before midnight the train steamed in. Jerszy lifted me to his shoulders again and plowed his way through the crowd once more. He sat me down on someone's suitcase in the corridor under the window, admonished me to silence, and disappeared in the crowd.

The whistle blew, doors slammed shut. Steam rose against the windows and the train rolled out of the station. I had no idea how long I had been on the road, what time or day it was. I sat on the suitcase barely able to grasp that I was now in Poland far away from where I had started. The people in the corridor were jammed together. Their faces were ashen and fear was in their eyes. They were fleeing the black menace. That much I understood. I wanted to be home. I thought about Mother. Had Father come home? Had Nora left yet? Were Lex and Mother all right? I felt as if I had no blood running through my veins anymore, just icy water.

Gdynia

The whistle blew and the train eased into Danzig, our first stop. The platform was full of German soldiers. Officials in black uniforms clustered around each wagon's door and forced passengers off the train. The corridor turned into a cacophony of shuffling feet and shrill voices. Soldiers instantly surrounded passengers who had been forced onto the platform. Unable to get away from the panicked crowd, I felt pursued by a thousand Obermeiers.

The pressure of people trying to get away forced me along the corridor and pushed me into an open compartment. A man pulled me in and immediately locked the door. An elegant, gray-haired woman patted a spot next to her. I sat down. My legs felt jointless.

The man picked up a German newspaper he had placed on the seat opposite the woman and continued reading where he must have left off when I fell in. The woman looked out the window and watched the swirling crowd. Her face was expressionless.

A heavy knock on the door made me jump. "Offnen," said a voice outside the door.

The man placed his paper on the seat, unlocked the door, and sat down again. An official in a German uniform stepped in.

"Papiere."

The man pulled papers out of the inside pocket of his coat and handed them to the official. The woman opened her purse and, without looking at the official, handed him her papers.

The official studied the papers, looked at the man and then at the papers again, making certain everything matched. When he was done, he returned the papers and the man picked up the newspaper and began to read again.

The woman looked out of the window while the official went through the same motions with her papers. He then turned to me.

"Papiere?"

My body froze into a solid piece of granite. Nothing functioned.

"Well?" I heard him say. His voice drifted into my head like smoke. Then everything cleared and I knew exactly what to do. I began to cry.

"I lost my mother," I wept out in German.

"Well, don't cry." He handed me a neatly folded blue handkerchief. I sobbed into it, blew my nose, and handed it back to him.

"You can keep it." His smile was reassuring.

"What's your name?"

I knew to use Mother's maiden name because it was German.

"Muller," I sputtered into the handkerchief.

"Well, we'll find her," he said in a consoling tone and stroked my cheek.

The woman turned from the window. "Don't disturb yourself, mein Herr. I will help her find her mother."

"Thank you, madam." The official made a quick, brief bow, marked the window by the door with a chalk cross, and left.

"I can find my mother myself," I said, afraid the woman might discover my lie.

In a low, conspiratorial voice she said, "I know you can."

Relieved of the fear of being discovered, I smiled at her.

"I am Mrs. Emmanuel and this is my husband." She extended her hand in a gesture of introduction. The man nodded over his newspaper.

A column of soldiers marched down the platform and dispersed through the train and swept more people off. The man in the lead noticed the chalk mark over our window, bowed, and went on.

People were herded out by rifle butts. Some staggered, and others fell. Nervously holding onto the seat, my throat like sand, I sat next to Mrs. Emmanuel, wishing the train would move. Mr. Emmanuel was hidden behind the newspaper.

Through the din I strained to hear the whistle that would signal the train to move. If the train did not move soon, the pounding of my heart would surely give me away. I turned away from the drama on the platform and watched Mr. Emmanuel's neatly manicured hands fold the paper. They were delicate, like a woman's, except for the tuft of hair on the back. The newspaper rustled while he tried to crease it. I could see now that his hands were shaking. He gave up and pretended to read it over again.

When the platform was empty, the whistle blew, and the conductor hung out the door and waved his paddle. At last, the train moved out on its way to Gdynia.

I released my grip on the seat. Mr. Emmanuel peeked over his newspaper and looked out. Mrs. Emmanuel sat quite still, her hands folded in her lap.

At Gdynia the train emptied. A porter came and carried Mr. and Mrs. Emmanuel's luggage. Without the cover of a crowd, I felt exposed. I kept close to the couple and stood undecided at the curb, watching their luggage being loaded into a black car. The chauffeur opened the door and Mrs. Emmanuel slid in.

I looked left and right and wondered where the wharf was. Uncertainty lay in my stomach like a boulder.

Mrs. Emmanuel leaned out of the car. "Do you know where to go?"

Her husband stood by the car door and turned to look at me. Before I could think up anything to say, he gently pushed me into the car, and then slid in beside me. He rapped on the window separating us from the chauffeur and the car eased away from the station. Apprehension ate at me. I had to get out of the car. I thought these people were hauling me off to a camp under the guise of kindness. I pulled and pushed at the car's door handle, but it would not budge. Mrs. Emmanuel took my hand. I pulled away.

"Don't be afraid. We'll get you to the wharf."

I wondered how she knew I had to be at the wharf. I was not convinced in spite of her gentle voice and her sad eyes. I thought about escape. I thought about my mother, who would never know what had happened to me.

Mr. Emmanuel sat with his hands cupping his knees and looked straight ahead.

"I'll get you there tomorrow," he said in a quiet voice Maybe they weren't Nazi spies.

Mrs. Emmanuel looked at me sadly.

"You need a bath," she said, and then, as if to soften the implication, she added, "And some food and sleep." She stroked my head.

Her gentle stroking of my head and the easy gliding of the car eased the urgency of getting to the wharf.

Their house was by the sea. I had not seen an ocean before and was awed and frightened by its thundering waves pounding against the land. A young woman in a white apron opened the beveled glass entry and welcomed us. Katja led me immediately to the bathroom and ordered me to undress while she filled the tub. She scrubbed me till I was raw. Wrapped in a Turkish towel, I sat at the kitchen table and drooled watching her fill a plate with fried potatoes and sausages. The white foam of the waves thundered against the retaining wall like a thousand marching feet.

I fell asleep in a luxurious bed and awakened to the sound of the sea and an overcast day. On the bed lay a neatly folded pile of new clothing. The aroma of frying eggs and sizzling bacon lured me to the kitchen. Katja was setting the table. She placed a full plate before me and bade me sit down. I took big bites from the bread and butter and wolfed down the eggs and bacon. Mrs. Emmanuel sat opposite me, her hands clasped on the table as if in prayer, and watched me eat. Through mouthfuls, I told her I had to be at the wharf at two o'clock.

Mr. Emmanuel stood by the buffet and sipped a cup of coffee. "I'll pick you up by one o'clock," he said, and slipped through the door.

Most of the morning I stood by the entry watching for Mr. Emmanuel. The sea roared against the retaining wall, and the thought of having to cross it terrified me.

At one o'clock sharp Mr. Emmanuel arrived.

Mrs. Emmanuel gave me a quick hug and Katja kissed me on the cheek. Again I felt a terrible sense of loss.

The car glided smoothly through the streets. Dark clouds threatened, but the streets were clear of snow. The cobblestones, polished by the shattering cold, glistened in the light of a pale sun. The wind blew from the sea, careening into people who fought for their footing.

At the wharf Mr. Emmanuel opened the door for me. I stood on the street and extended my hand to him. He squeezed it so hard I had to hold back tears.

"Good luck," he said with his sad smile and turned to the chauffeur. I watched the black car glide down the cobblestones and disappear around a turn.

Huge tankers and ships were berthed at the wharf. Small fishing and sailboats rocked in the waves around the big ships, like moths drawn to light.

Blasted by the wind I sat on the wharf, my new coat wrapped around me, my scarf over my mouth. My feet dangling over the edge of the wall, I surveyed the myriad of boats tossed by the waves. Often I would rise and wander over to a dockworker to ask the time.

A small fishing boat rocked toward the wharf. A man dressed in a yellow fisherman's slicker and hat stood on the deck, drenched by the foaming waves. He cupped his hands around his mouth and shouted across the roar of the waves. "Czeziiiiiiin." The wind blew the long sound over the wall.

I stood and waved with both hands and yelled back. "Czeziiiiiin." The fisherman whipped the boat around the hull of a huge tanker and guided it to where I stood. He stopped at the high wall that kept the sea from invading the town. The boat bobbed up and down. As I looked down on it from the height of the wall, its rocking motion made me dizzy.

"Come," the fisherman yelled into the wind and waved both hands.

No steps led down to the sea. "How?" I yelled back.

"Jump! Jump!"

I took a step forward, closed my eyes, and jumped. When I hit the deck, my feet slipped away from me and I landed on my back. The boat rocked ominously. I kept slipping and falling when I tried to rise, and finally just sat on the wet deck not caring about anything. The fisherman helped me up and led me to his bunk.

Gales tossed the boat and waves sprayed the porthole. Dark clouds fermented overhead. The fisherman negotiated the choppy waters of the Baltic to Sweden's coast, while I lay on his bunk and vomited into a paper sack.

He tied his boat up at the beach in Solvesborg, took my hand, and led me on my shaky legs to a white house with a red roof that seemed to sprout out of a sand dune.

His wife, Inga, embraced me. She had a roundness similar to that of the farmer's wife in Czechoslovakia. I do not remember how long I stayed. I had no notion of the time and distance I had traveled when I arrived at Inga's house, but I knew I did not want to leave. My past was gone, and my future loomed like an abysmal void.

The day we parted I cried. I clung to Inga as if she were a teddy bear.

"There, there. You're all right now. There will be no more Germans."

I cried more. Inga wiped my tears with her apron. It smelled of fish.

Bjork, the fisherman, and Inga took me to the train station.

They chatted all the way to the station. I did not understand a word, but the sounds were of encouragement. When the train chugged out on its way to Goteborg, I leaned out of the morning train, glued to the image of Inga's receding figure, and waved the blue handkerchief the German official had given me in Danzig.

Within a week of arriving in Goteborg I sailed across the temperamental North Sea on the passenger ship *Suecia*.

My stomach rolled with the sea. I was unable to eat any of the food laid out for us. I vomited till there was nothing left to vomit and spent five days lying on my bunk, certain that I was dying. The *Suecia* docked in Southampton in May, two months after the Germans had marched into Prague, and two months before my thirteenth birthday.

1939 — 1945

England

Anxious to get ground under my feet, I wove down the heaving ramp of the *Suecia* holding on to both sides of the ropes guiding me to the dock.

A group of children huddled by the wharf's edge. My legs were unsure, and my stomach collapsed with the emptiness of vomiting and lack of food as I listed toward them. A uniformed official attempted to line us up. We followed him in a disorderly fashion to a table set up on the dock.

A rosy-cheeked woman with translucent skin and a crinkly smile asked my name, wrote it on a piece of cardboard, and looped the tag through my lapel with string. My back to the wind, I stepped aside and watched the tagging with little interest.

When everyone was labeled, the uniformed man led us to a train and loaded us like baggage into several compartments.

Hungry, sick, and tired, I hardly cared where I was going. Dunes and downs and houses floated by like a hazy dream.

At Victoria Station in London, we were unloaded and hauled off to a hostel, where I had a bath, ate my first meal in five days, and fell into a sound sleep between clean sheets.

The following day, a woman dressed in a tweed suit walked me through streets covered with black fog. Lamps shed a dull sepia glow that formed weak pools of light on an invisible street. Her flashlight guided us one slow step at a time. The hall of the station was brightly lit and the people on the platform milled around casually and unperturbed, while I kept looking behind me for a column of soldiers to round us all up. The strange sound of the language, the different looking streets, the unaccustomed color of the official uniforms kept me in a constant state of anxiety.

The woman marched down the platform, resolutely swinging her arms like some sergeant leading troops. I tried to keep up with her but was slowed by the visceral feeling that a troop of men with red armbands on their sleeves was momentarily going to march in and apprehend us. The woman kept urging me to hurry, but I limped along, looking behind me. She finally walked back toward me, took me by the hand, and pulled me along. She found an empty compartment that seemed to suit her and led me to a seat, handed me a paper sack, took out a slip of paper from her purse, and wrote something on it. I watched her mouth the word "Carlisle."

She looked at me intently. "Carlisle," she repeated.

I nodded. She smiled, patted me on my knee, and left. I had no more idea where Carlisle was than I had known where Katowice or Goteborg was, nor did I have any idea in which direction I was traveling. There was no end of unknown places in the world. I seemed destined to spend my life traveling on trains or on foot from town to village with no permanent place to land. I belonged nowhere.

Events had progressed so quickly that I had no time to understand their implications. As I sat in the luxury of a compartment totally my own, a slow anger began to ooze into my veins. I wanted to have a say about my life, about where I wanted to go and what I wanted to do. I wanted to pinpoint the reason why I was here, and tried to remember just how it had all started, but only a confusion of images, of towns and landscapes mingled through my head and nameless people passed through my memory like shadows.

New landscapes sped by: green pastures of lush grass neatly parceled by hedges dividing one from another, gardens attached to bungalows like colorful aprons. This then was England where my mother believed me to be safe, but I did not feel safe. I felt as if I were skimming across a thin sheet of crackling ice that was going to give way any moment and send me plunging into an abyss of darkness to drown.

The sensation of hunger broke through the feeling of anger and frustration. I examined the brown paper bag. There were two curiously thin slices of white bread cut into triangles covering some unknown greens. Later I would learn that it was watercress. Concentrating on the strange, soft white bread and the sharp flavor of the greens I forgot, for a moment, my misery.

I had left in March and now it was May. My mother had said she would be in England within a month. The happy thought, that she had arrived before I had, lifted my spirits. Where would she be? How could I find out? Would she be able to find me?

Except for the stationmaster, the platform in Carlisle was deserted. The wind kept swatting my nametag into my face as I scanned the empty platform. A woman appeared and walked toward me with a determined stride. She wore tweeds and sturdy shoes. Pince-nez dangled from a gold chain and swung back and forth across her flat chest.

She stepped abruptly in front of me, lifted her pince-nez and looked me over, then lifted my nametag and studied it.

"Refugee Darvasova?" she queried in a pinched tone.

Actually my name was Darvas. In the Slavic countries the "ova" tagged onto a name means "belonging to." Since I did not belong to anyone, and my first name was not "Refugee," I corrected her.

"Miriam Darvas."

"Ah, good. And where is your luggage?"

I shrugged. I didn't understand her.

"You mean you don't know?"

I shrugged again.

She turned to a porter who stood at some distance watching us with mild interest. "Come here," she said.

The porter strolled toward her and tipped his hat as he approached. She asked him something in clipped syllables.

He shrugged. "No luggage."

"No luggage?" The woman clucked her tongue.

I learned the word "luggage" that day.

She indicated for me to follow her to a waiting car, slid in the back seat and instructed the chauffeur to drive.

She chattered as I sat in perplexed silence. Then she pointed at herself and in precisely enunciated words, she said, "My name is Miss Masters." I nodded.

The car slid through a wrought iron gate. A shiny brass plate emblazoned with the word "Nazdar" announced the entry to Miss Masters's estate.

What was the familiar Czech word for "so long" doing at the end of the world? Later I learned that Miss Masters had been to Prague twice. She had memorialized her visits with the brass sign, but it was the only Czech word she knew.

The house stood on the crest of a hill, against dark trees rising into a hazy May sky. The view from its windows, which I came to know well, was of emerald meadows, lush and brilliant, gliding into distant blue-black woods. The nearer gardens were manicured lawns defined by the red and lavender blossoms of vibrant rhododendron shrubs. Beyond the circular cobblestone courtyard and through the woods, willows encircled a lake. It was fed by Eden Brook, which flowed through the village of Brampton. A narrow arched bridge led to a small island covered with azaleas and rhododendron. In time, this would become my favorite spot. I would sit hidden from view amid the greenery and wonder about what would happen next.

The first few days at Nazdar were indescribably lonely. I wandered aimlessly through echoing halls, smiled at the servants, and sat silently across the table from Miss Masters and watched her strange ritual of eating.

With her knife, she pressed her food against the back of her fork tines and guided it expertly to her mouth. My attempts at this new eating method failed. I could not keep the food on the tines without losing it so I continued to shovel the food into the hollow of my fork in spite of Miss Masters's gentle attempts to change the habit. The afternoon tea with tiny watercress and cucumber sandwiches was yet another ritual at which we sat across from each other in silence. Miss Masters's attempts at conversation became a series of monologues. I responded with a steady gaze while I continued to eat the bite-size sandwiches and concentrated on the novel texture of white bread and the crunch of the cucumbers.

That summer I was immersed in learning English. Mr. Hunt, my tutor, was a jovial round gentleman. His bald head with white tufts of hair above each ear made him look like an oversized elf. At first I steeled myself for a battle with him. His appearance must be deceiving, I thought. Obermeier's had been. But Mr. Hunt's appearance was in keeping with his personality. He was a gentle man.

He coaxed me, encouraged me, and approved of everything I did. I looked forward to his coming, and yet I was burdened with not knowing whether or not my mother had arrived in England. I tried to ask Miss Masters about her, but did not have the words to make myself understood. I asked in German, but received blank looks. I tried in Czech and French, but received the same blank stares.

Life took on a routine. Before breakfast Miss Masters and I would take a brisk hike into the woods. The tips of the trees were soft salmon sunshine. The meadows were white with daisies, and the rhododendron trailed a line of crimson along the edge of the lawn.

A breakfast of kippers followed after the hike. I hated kippers. Since I did not care whether or not my food stayed on my fork when I ate them, I practiced the correct English manner of eating with fork tines down, and thus managed not to get any kippers in my mouth.

After breakfast, I walked up the wide curving stairs to the library. The darkly paneled room was encircled by shelves of books from floor to ceiling. I studied there till Mr. Hunt arrived at ten sharp. The lessons always started and ended on a happy note.

"Hello, my dear, and a good morning to you." His greeting was the same each morning and so was his smile.

"And a good morning to you, too," I had learned to reply.

I learned to speak English after a fashion. My "r" was the Czech alveolar trill. I pronounced the "w" as a "v" as the Germans do, and the "on" endings as French nasals. My emphasis was usually on the wrong syllable, demanding careful attention from the listener.

By four o'clock, I was free to do as I pleased. I wandered to the pond and watched the sun sparkle on its shimmering surface. On Saturdays, I ambled along the brook through the woods and pastures to the village of Eden or Brampton, and as I walked I worried about my mother and sister and thought about all that was gone from my life. I had no emotional attachment that could sustain me and wondered whether I would go through life dogged by anxiety, uncertainty, and anger.

After dinner, I read the newspaper to Miss Masters.

"It will improve your English," Miss Masters said, and corrected every word I pronounced.

At last I could ask the question that had occupied my mind through Mr. Hunt's teaching and Miss Masters's monologues.

"Where can I find out about my mother?"

"Write to the Society of Friends, they might know. And write to your mother."

"But she will not get the letter, if she is here."

"If she has left, the letter will be returned."

What if it were returned because she had been arrested? Would it have "address unknown" written on it?

The Society of Friends sent me Mother's new address in Prague and Nora's address in Sussex. I didn't know where that was, but I learned that she and Chris had arrived together and were on a farm. I immediately wrote to mother to tell her that Nora and Chris had arrived safely and sent their address. Nora was a lazy correspondent and seldom answered my letters. When she finally did write, it was to tell me in succinct words that a car had killed Chris.

My anger at the world grew. It was not the car that had killed Chris, but the men who had forced him out of his home. I wanted so desperately to avenge him, and my father, and Kurt, but my utter helplessness in the face of all this power burned more anger into my veins and smoldered within me like hot cinders.

I ran to the post office daily and came away disappointed. I received no reply from my mother.

When I did not hear from Mother, I imagined that she had been arrested and worried about what they might do to her and Lex. I was unable to eat or concentrate on my studies. I was drowning in my terror and my loneliness.

The rumblings in Europe were distant and unreal in the solitude of Nazdar. Life around me seemed to stand still.

"You'll hear from her, you'll see," Mr. Hunt assured me. His words were prophetic. The following day a letter arrived from my mother. I was so excited I ran to the island and hid in the rhododendron bushes where I could be alone to savor every line of that familiar handwriting.

July 27, 1939
My dear Miriam,

I was overjoyed to hear that you arrived safely and that you were not afraid. I am enclosing a few stamps from your album. You will have to buy a book for them since I cannot send yours. We are not allowed to send valuables out of the country.

Soon you will be going to school, and I hope that you will apply yourself and study diligently. But by then I will be with you. I hope that I will soon receive permission to leave. I am constantly running from the Gestapo to a committee for my papers.

I hope that you are happy and that you are not only learning to speak English but other things as well, so that you will become a good human being.

Many kisses, Mutti

I was overwhelmed with a sense of forgotten warmth and filled with hope and anticipation for a reunion, and I waited eagerly for her next letter. While I waited, my emotional balance teetered back and forth between hope and despair.

The next letter arrived a month after her first letter.

August 8, 1939
My dear Miriam,

I have received your two letters and am shocked to hear that a car killed Chris. It upset me particularly, because you said he had successfully made the trip from Prague, only to die in safety.

I was so terribly nervous about Nora, and am relieved she is with a family. Where is Sussex?

I am still running around for my papers and am at the point of despair. Everything costs a great deal of money, and I do not know where to get any more. I am doing everything to be with you as soon as possible. It is getting progressively harder to get a traveling permit. Tomorrow I am again going quite a distance to Dejvice, where the Gestapo Headquarters is. I hope the Gestapo will give me permission to leave. I would very much like to be with you.

Many kisses, Mutti

I visualized the black uniforms and the black boots my mother had to confront and became so anxious that I could not sleep. I was on the verge of tears most of the time. Her next letter did not lift my spirits.

August 9, 1939
My dear Miriam,

I just arrived home from the Gestapo Headquarters in Dejvice and can tell you that I have all my papers. They are now, along with my passport, at the Gestapo. I was told that I would have permission to leave within ten days. You cannot imagine how much running around I had to do, how much money all this cost. My nerves are stretched to the breaking point. I was in such despair at times that I gave up hope of ever getting out of here. Now, all I have to do is get the ticket, as Miss W., who was supposed to supply the ticket, has used it for her return trip to England. I don't know to whom to turn. Perhaps you could call the Society of Friends and find out who will arrange for another ticket for me. I am such a nervous wreck from all this running around and confusion that I cannot write properly. I am now going to make another trip to yet another agency about the ticket. If I get it, then you will not have to do anything. I will let you know immediately. Don't do anything yet. Am enclosing stamps again.

Many kisses, Mutti

I was desperate. There was no telephone at Nazdar. How was I going to help my mother? I asked Miss Masters.

"Your mother will manage. You'll see."

This was of no help. How could she be indifferent, I thought, when my mother's life was at stake?

I answered Mother and told her that I would do anything she told me to do. When her next letter arrived, I tore it open, hoping she was telling me that she was on the way.

August 30, 1939

My dear Miriam,

Received your letter. I have now everything for the trip but the money. The Society of Friends, the English consulate, everybody has left. You must get in touch with the Society of Friends in London. But you have to work fast, otherwise I will not be able to get out of here anymore. The political situation is getting desperate and people are no longer able to get out. Try your best to get to London, but for heaven's sake don't cry, don't lose your head. You cannot help that way. I would have liked to spare you all this, but there is no other way out. You cannot imagine how much all this has taken out of me, and now at the last minute and after all the effort, I cannot get out. Yesterday I had to pay out one hundred and thirty-five crowns for duty. Today I must pay another two hundred to expedite matters. This, however, should be the last of the payments I will have to make. All the expense, the running around, the nerves! Now the whole thing is collapsing because I cannot get my ticket. It is driving me to despair. I am naturally going to do my utmost, but the best thing to do is to get in touch with the Society of Friends in London. I have also written to the Committee for Refugees in London. They have sent me a permit to enter England. I am so nervous I cannot write anymore. So, don't cry. Try to arrange something with the Committee for Refugees or the Society of Friends.

Many kisses, Mutti

Misgivings covered me like a wet blanket under which I could hardly breathe.

I asked Miss Masters how I could get to London.

"My dear, that is a day's trip by train."

Since I had no money, a train trip was not an option. I tore a sheet of paper out of my workbook, and wrote:

Dear Society of Friends,

My mother needs your help. She has all her papers including the permit to enter England, but cannot get a ticket for the trip, because she has no money left. Would you please help her? Her name is Mathilde Darvas and her address is na Porici 10, Prague.

Thank you,
Miriam Darvas

Miss Masters addressed and stamped the envelope and the chauffeur drove it to the village post office. I waited impatiently for a timely reply, but did not receive one.

On September 3, 1939, Britain and France declared war on Germany. Two months later, I finally received a letter from my mother. It was to be my last.

November 11, 1939
My dear Miriam,

I was very happy to hear from you. I thought that perhaps we would not be able to write to each other anymore, but your letter did come through. I am afraid we will not be able to see one another again till the war is over. Don't despair, my darling. I will always be with you in my heart and my thoughts. I hope you will be able to catch up on your schooling. Is the climate very bad?

That you like it there is a good sign and pleases me. I am calmer knowing that you like it, but then you are a big girl now, and with sense one can live anywhere. Learn English well. It is a world language and will serve you well throughout your life.

I am well. Lex was released from prison and we now share my small apartment. If he had not been released, I would have literally starved to death, since I had spent all my money on papers and bribes. We do not know what has happened to Steffie or your father. Needless to say, we are both quite upset, but at least we can share our grief.

I have some very painful news for you. Angelika and her parents were arrested last night. I hesitated to tell you, but then decided that you need to know. I could not even say good-bye to them. I wonder when they will come for Lex and me.

I have signed up at the library and sit at home with a book most of the time. You know that cold weather has never agreed with me. At the moment it is spring-like here, and I have dared to go out. I am content, and will spend the months ahead waiting to see you again. So, study diligently and be sensible, so that I will be proud of you.

Many kisses, Mutti

I realized that I was quite alone, without family, without possessions, without hope. I knew that the Germans wanted Lex because he had been arrested before; I knew my mother was probably on the Gestapo's list because she had been married to a wanted man. For several days I hid in the rhododendron bushes on the island and made up rescue scenes.

Miss Masters kept asking me what the matter was but I refused to answer her questions. But when Mr. Hunt asked in his soft, caressing voice I blurted out:

"My mother cannot come to England and the Germans arrested my friend in Prague and my friend Chris was killed by a car."

"There, there. Let's you and I go for a walk to the village."

On the way to Eden I told him about my father and mother, Angelika and Chris, Steffie and Lex. Mr. Hunt nodded and from time to time he stroked my hair. By the time we had walked back, I had talked myself out.

"You'll always have your parents and your friends."

"I'll never see them again."

"They will be in your memory and your heart. So long as they are remembered, they live. Your mother is safe. You'll see her again."

I did not want to have them as memories. I wanted them in the flesh, here and now. Who were these Nazis, this Gestapo, this Hitler who were in such relentless pursuit of my family for no reason I could understand? The smoldering anger in my veins turned to a fury of frustration. I wanted to kill them all but I felt chained, incapable of doing anything against this might of machines and men.

My dream and my hope had been to meet Mother on the

platform at Wilson station in Prague. I would run to her and fall into her arms and smell that faint scent of mimosa that surrounded her. Then she would look at me surprised and say, "You have grown into a young woman. I am so proud of you." Arm in arm we would walk down Vaclavske namesti and talk and talk. I had to somehow resign myself to not seeing her again. I fought against it, but life went about its ordained course without any direction from me.

When the chestnut trees had dropped their fruit and the rhododendron blooms were done, I found myself sitting again in Miss Masters's car, in sad silence. I was being shipped to Brighton & Hove Public Girls' School. Why I was being sent from the border of Scotland to the tip of southern England was not explained to me.

I watched Nazdar disappear through the rear window of Miss Masters's Rolls Royce. Mist hung over the hill and blurred the sharp outlines of the manor into soft strokes of gray.

I turned to Miss Masters. "I don't want to go to girls' school."

"Now, we have gone through that."

She had earlier explained, after my objection to leaving, that I could always spend holidays with her. "And besides, you have the opportunity to become something."

I did not know what one was when one became something. I had no choice in any case. As the train pulled out, I leaned out of the window and waved good-bye. Miss Masters stood on the platform and waved her lacy handkerchief. She dabbed at her eyes from time to time. I hung out the window till the lacy handkerchief was cut from view by-swells of hills and trees, and a new knot of anxiety melted into the walls of my veins. I did not see Miss Masters again.

I settled into the train compartment and listened to the familiar sound of the wheels. Like a transitory bird detached from her flock, I had no familiar place to land. From this moment I insulated myself against pain. Life was going to be a series of encounters without attachments to anyone or anything.

At Brighton & Hove Public Girls' School—public in England means private—I was assigned to Lower Four B. I did not know what that meant.

My dorm assignment was a cot under the attic window overlooking the sea. My two roommates, Prunella and Vivian, were annoying shadows dimming my existence. They considered me worthy of their malevolent pranks. They hid my books, blotched ink stains over neatly written workbooks, and laughed at my mispronunciation.

Miss Winton, the headmistress and English teacher, assigned Shylock's speech from Shakespeare's *Merchant of Venice* for me to memorize.

My understanding of what Shakespeare had to say was nil, nor could I pronounce the "th" he attached to endings of words. Beryl, a sympathetic classmate, offered to help me memorize Shylock's speech in return for two weeks of my desserts.

We sat on the wet sand by the waves of the Channel while Beryl read. "I have possess'd your grace of what I purpose; and by our holy Sabbath..." I imitated each sound with the undaunted ignorance of a parrot.

On the day of my recital, I stood on the podium of Lower Four B and rattled off Shylock's speech, having not the vaguest notion what I was saying. The girls of Lower Four B sat in surprised silence.

When I had finished, Miss Winton applauded and remarked to the class how conscientious foreigners were. She awarded me the gold star. My status improved that day and my schoolbooks no longer disappeared.

In physics I learned the word "velocity." I liked the sound, but its meaning escaped me.

The anger that was oozing through my veins now evidenced itself in resentment against any authority, and I had problems with the rules of how to wear the pea green uniform. The blazer with the golden crest on the left breast was to be buttoned at all times. The round, bowler-like hat with its two-inch brim was to be worn two fingers up from the bridge of the nose so that the crest above the brim was centered. The bloomers, with elastic round the legs, were to be worn pulled to the knee during gym, but pushed up the thigh beneath a skirt. The pale gold and green horizontally striped tie was to be knotted in a Windsor knot and centered on the pale gold shirt. I resented Miss Winton's constant reprimands about my appearance.

She hopped along the corridors on thin legs like a flightless bird. Secretly we called her Dodo. The sound of her hopping allowed the girls to avoid her, but I had not yet developed that knack. She seemed to hop out of corners to catch me with a reprimand for my slovenly appearance.

"Your hat is altogether at too rakish an angle."

I understood "hat" but the words "rakish" and "angle" eluded me, Since I was not certain what she wanted, but understood that it was some order or another, I smiled and walked away. She cornered me after class and, with an annoyed expression, straightened my hat. By the time she criticized me for my incorrectly knotted tie, I had learned the rudiments necessary for understanding reprimands but chose to ignore them.

I looked at my tie. It seemed in order to me and besides, I was going to wear it the way I wanted.

"Have someone show you how to tie it," she clucked, and hopped away.

At other times my blazer was not buttoned or my bloomers were in evidence. I ignored it all and when I dressed, I perversely forgot the rules.

"I was too rushed," I would explain on my next encounter with Miss Winton.

"Start getting ready earlier" was her curt reply.

The regiment of rising at five in the morning for calisthenics, the four-minute cold showers, the crowding into the big hall for "Our Father Who Art in Heaven" sung before breakfast to Miss Winton's piano playing chafed me. My rebellion was definite and intentional. I spent many days under house arrest in a small room furnished with a cot and blanket, no pillow, no window. Someone had tacked a picture of Jesus over the cot and I would spend hours contemplating his plight and mine. I was alone and persecuted, but I was not nailed to a cross. Like Voltaire's *Candide*, I consoled myself with the thought that things could be worse.

After the hymn-singing in the mornings, the race to the dining hall was on. The crowding and jostling of the disorderly stampede were too reminiscent of past upheavals, reminding me of the panicked people hanging from streetcars and pushing into railway stations. I hung back to avoid it till I learned that the last in line got the least food.

The dining hall was a clatter of plates and trays as the unruly line moved forward. The daily porridge was slopped into a bowl and crowned with a soggy piece of toast. By the time I reached my seat at the table, the mush was jostled out of the bowl, its quivering mass oozing onto the tray. At first I ate only what was left in the bowl. To avoid hunger pangs long before lunch, I learned to scoop the slopped mess back into the bowl. Soon I ate the slopped mess directly from the tray and scraped off every last bit with my soggy toast.

A brisk barter system developed among those who received food packages from home. I had nothing to trade and went to bed hungry. I regretted trading my dessert for Beryl's coaching. The importance of the gold star receded when my stomach growled.

On Sundays and holidays, the esplanade hugging the shore was resplendent with colors. Women strolled along the walk in filmy summer dresses carrying sun-flecked parasols. Children scampered gaily among the ramparts. Young people flocked into the amusement arcade. A group of spectators listened to the Brighton band perched on the edge of the pier under an arched bandstand.

I sat on the pier dangling my legs above the English Channel the way I had done sitting on the wharf on the Baltic. Spots of sunlight danced upon the rippled silver sheet of water. I studied it and wondered how my mother and Lex were doing and if they were still all right.

Soon coils of concertina wire were rolled along the beach and blocked access. Fascinated by the sea, I sauntered along the wire, shoes in hand, wet sand squashing through my toes. Silvery drops of light sparkled on the surface beyond the foamy waves. Flotsam from British merchant ships that had been sunk by German torpedoes was deposited on the beach by the rambling waves: sodden boxes of food, tins of tea. I saw pencils bobbing in the waves like bright yellow sea urchins playing hide and seek.

The sea's perpetual motion and constantly changing color enraptured me. Its glittering surface on calm days and the spumous froth of its waves and its roaring anger on stormy days held an endless wonder.

At night the fire of antiaircraft guns blazed crimson against the dark sky, changing the restless sea into pools of molten copper.

The war had come too close to Brighton.

On a foggy November day, parents arrived to take their daughters to shelter and I was once more whisked off. "To Wales," Miss Winton said, but she might as well have said "to the moon." I resented being told to leave once more and actually thought about just leaving on my own. But I knew neither in which direction to go nor how to get anywhere. The not knowing I resented, too. The anger was now sizzling like acid through my whole body.

I found myself in the village of Denbigh, where the ruin of Denbigh Castle rose on a hill. Grasses swayed in the breeze around the mossy stones and rolling knolls like a restless sea. I lived in a youth hostel filled with refugees from various European countries. I learned about their individual tragedies. Each story diminished mine but did not diminish my anger.

One day, I walked away from the rules. I wandered along deserted country roads going wherever they would take me. I climbed fences to cross green meadows dotted with grazing cows and kept walking till I discovered the town of Rhyl. I bought a tuppenny ice cream bar and sat on the beach facing the Irish Sea and watched the boats sailing across the ocean. Perhaps they carried someone like me to some unknown place. Perhaps I could get into one of those boats and ask the fisherman to take me back to where I came from. But at dusk I realized that I did need a roof over my head. I had no idea where Denbigh was, and I asked a policeman for directions.

"That's a distance, girl."

"Which way?"

"You can't walk that."

"But I did."

"Too dark now. You won't find your way."

"I will."

"Come on, I'll take you."

He hopped on his bicycle and lifted me onto its handlebars. We wobbled down dark country roads illuminated only by his bicycle lamp. He led me into the hall of the old villa where I was immediately surrounded by a gaggle of adults wanting to know where I had been. I remained silent.

"I found her in Rhyl," the policeman explained.

"Rhyl! How did you manage that?" Mr. Purdy wanted to know.

"I walked."

"That's not possible."

"I did," I said. Annoyed with his questioning the truth of my statement, I walked away.

"No harm done," said the policeman, coming to my aid.

A few days later I sat again in a train compartment on my way to a new hostel in Kettering. I spent long enough in that hostel to read its modest library of German books. Alone and undisturbed, I sat in the small, musty room and waded through Grimmelhausen's seventeenth-century tome on the Thirty Years' War, *Simplizius Simplicissimus*. I empathized with Simplizius. He had lost his parents and his homeland in the Thirty Years' War, wandered restlessly from place to place, and learned about the vagaries of politics and war. At least his tragedy was recorded. Mine was unrecorded and insignificant on the vast canvas of life.

By the time I was on a train again traveling south to Long Dene school—with no idea how the decisions to send me hither and yon had been arrived at, nor by whom—I had become inured to leave-taking. In the two years I had spent in England, I had seen as much of that country as I had seen of Germany, Czechoslovakia, Austria, and France. Having met innumerable refugees, I had learned that life was the history of individual tragedies.

I arrived at Windsor on a hot summer day. No one was there to meet me. I walked to Stoke Poges where I asked a man for directions to Long Dene School, an old manor house, in Slough.

"It's that-a-way," he said, pointing in the direction of a field.

Carrying my small suitcase, bought by Miss Masters, I walked down tree-lined streets and past fields, stopping now and then to ask if I was on the right road. The road finally turned into a dusty path. In the middle of the path stood a man who seemed to be waiting for me. This was John Guinness, the headmaster. He took my suitcase and led me to a sparsely furnished room with two beds, a chest of drawers, a desk, and chair.

"The others will arrive next week," he said. "Two Czechs will be among them, a brother and sister." He put the suitcase on the bed.

"May I choose my roommate?"

"I thought you might want the Czech student."

"That would be nice," I said. "What's her name?"

"Lilka. Her brother's name is Teo." He turned to leave.

Though the prospect of two compatriots thrilled me, I was hungry. "When is dinner?" I said.

He turned back. "Dinner at seven," he said, and left.

I walked to the bare window and looked out across a courtyard into a hot, dusty field. I was happy at the prospect of having a Czech roommate.

Around seven, I crossed the lawn to the main building in search of the dining room. I met no one and was wondering which way to turn, when John Guinness appeared. While waiting for the dining room to open, he showed me the various rooms and asked me about myself. I did not answer his questions and he did not press me further. In the years I spent at Long Dene, I never heard John issue an order. Nor did he demand that the rules be followed to the letter. He did once say that rules and laws are not chiseled into stone, and that we must learn to use our judgment. I liked him. He was the first person I allowed myself to develop an attachment to. For a while, the burning anger in my veins was dampened.

I needed no coaxing to go barefoot, to eat Jerusalem artichokes and walnut meat loaf, to choose academic subjects to my liking, and go to the dining room whenever I wanted. There were always leftovers.

The following week, John and I stood on the platform waiting for the train to pull in. Noisy, young people tumbled onto the platform. I searched the faces for Lilka and Teo.

A tall girl with an upturned nose and a full mouth jumped from the train. She had feline blue eyes and porcelain skin. Her blonde hair hung down the center of her back in a heavy braid. Behind her came a perfect masculine image of the girl, a boy with the same easy smile. She greeted John with that smile and shook his hand. I knew instantly that this was Lilka and Teo and immediately fell in love.

Lilka thought that Miriam was too long and formal a name and called me Mirka. I liked it.

It was a most beautiful summer that year. The school was full of laughter and fun, and I felt less anxiety than I had for some time. Generally, everybody did as he pleased, which was the credo of the school.

Lilka and I became friends. I fell in love with Teo.

Teo and I would meet in Windsor at Lyon's Corner House, have tea, and then dawdle through the fields hand in hand back to school. Sometimes we explored the countryside; sometimes we lay in the warm fields. Inexplicable feelings raced through my body when we held each other close.

Anthony, a lanky, wild-eyed, dark-haired boy, fell in love with Lilka, and Lilka adored him. He saw in the connection between pupil and professor a master-slave relationship analogous to the oppression of the proletariat by their capitalist exploiters. I thought him mad.

Toward the end of those lazy, beautiful summer weeks, Lilka confided to me that she had found her womanhood down by the pond among the rhododendron.

"Not with Anthony," I said.

"But I love him," Lilka said.

"He's mad."

"No, he's not." Flushed with anger she turned to me. "He is politically more aware than anyone. Is that being mad?"

"I suppose not." I was not convinced, however. But I left the subject of Anthony alone.

The war was distant. An occasional plane passed overhead, and we could hear the air raid sirens warning of danger. From the newspaper we learned what was happening and we cheered a battle won and moaned when disaster struck somewhere. We knew of London being bombed, and though it was not far, the danger did not reach us. The war seemed remote in this semi-secure world of academics.

Suddenly it was our last term before graduation. The air was redolent with the warm smell of spring. The breeze caressed our bodies as Teo and I lay in each other's arms in the grasses by the brook. There was magic in the air and I wished these days would last forever. Teo rose on his elbow and looked toward the sky where a plane trailed a cotton white streak across the horizon.

"I'm going to be in one of those and bomb the Germans to hell."

"How are you going to do that?"

"I'm going to join the Air Force."

I knew that Teo would be going to war, but the statement

stabbed me with the force of an ice pick and stopped my breath. I wanted everything to stay just as it was and had pushed the thought of Teo's departure into the dark recesses of my mind, hoping for forgetfulness.

The magic in the air slipped away like ether. The sense of loss that had embedded itself in my body exploded into tears of anger and pain.

"Hey, don't cry. I can finally do something about the Nazis."

"Well, I can't. I'm not allowed to fight."

"You will fight in a different way, you'll see."

I did not want to fight in a different way. I wanted to be a fighter pilot. Fat chance.

We walked arm in arm back to school, both deep in thought.

I found Lilka sitting on her bed crying into a wad of toilet paper.

"Anthony is joining the Air Force," she blurted, and blew her nose.

I sat down beside her, put my arms around her, and cried with her.

The last month of our stay was a roller coaster. Lilka and I were eagerly anticipating our graduation, but the joy was overcast with the sadness of having to part from Teo and Anthony.

The day after we graduated from Long Dene School, Teo and Anthony left for the Air Force. The whole school accompanied them to the station and sent them off with shouts of "good luck." Handkerchiefs and scarves waved through the air with riotous cheers and again I watched a train disappear into the distance. Life was good-byes, remembrance, and sadness.

Our futures were to be decided the day of Teo's departure at a conference with John Guinness.

"They're going to ship us somewhere, you'll see," Lilka said.

"I'm not going."

"You can't just say you won't go."

"Watch me."

I was resolute. I would never again go anywhere that I did not want to go. I knew what I wanted: to study history at London University. I wanted to comprehend the events that created this war and gave rise to Hitler with his despotic hold over countries and peoples.

We sat before John Guinness. I was sullen and unresponsive, prepared to hear that I was again being shipped off somewhere. I was so preoccupied with planning my rebellion that I did not hear what he said.

"I'm going to London to university," I interrupted.

There was a momentary silence.

"That's what you want to do?"

It was a fine day and the garden was beginning to burst into color. I did not want to leave this place, yet I knew I must.

"I'm not going anywhere you are going to send me."

"I'm not sending you anywhere. I'm asking you what you want to do."

I had steeled myself for a battle and there was none.

"Well, what do you want to do?" he asked me.

"I want to go to the university in London and study history."

"Fine. History is a fine subject. I'll get the papers ready."

I could not believe that it was so simple.

"Are you sure?"

"You can go wherever you want."

"I'm going, too," Lilka said.

We had discussed going together, but Lilka had left it up to me to force the issue.

"What do you want to study?"

"Art."

"That's good."

I jumped up and hugged Lilka and John and twirled out of the room into the garden and lay down on the turf. The sky was its murky English blue and the scent from the blooms of spring filled the air and I was happy.

Lilka lay down beside me. We held hands, looked at the sky and talked about what it would be like to do finally what we chose to do and to go where we chose to go.

We both hoped that London would bring Teo and Anthony back into our lives. It was, after all, easier to get to than Slough was.

It was not easy to say good-bye to John. We solemnly shook hands. He held mine for some time, then put his other hand over mine.

"I wish you success and joy," he said and looked at me with a sadness that was contagious.

Lilka threw her arms around his neck and cried. I wanted to cry, too, but I would not let myself.

John saw us off at the station. When the train moved around the curve at which we used to cross to go to Windsor, he vanished from sight as so many before him had done.

Sadness was soon replaced by eager anticipation. We would reunite with Teo and Anthony when they would come to London for their furlough, we hoped. Lilka and I boisterously sang old Czech songs and new English ones, trying to shout over the train's loud clack-clack.

London

With stipend money from the Czech-British Refugees Trust Fund assured, and a shared, new suitcase from Woolworth's in our hands, Lilka and I made the trip from Long Dene School to London.

We stepped uneasily into an atmosphere of uncertainty and suspense and were unprepared for shattered houses and piles of rubble and intimidated by the reality of something we had only read about. Taking turns lugging our suitcase, we walked through fog and passed perilously leaning walls amid ashes and smoke. Placards tacked to gutted walls announced "Beware the secret weapon!"

At our assigned hostel in Holborn, we were issued gas masks and asked if we would join the ARP (Air Raid Post). We did, and had brief training in the use of the gas masks by being forced to crawl through a huge corrugated tin culvert filled with smoke. I came out at the other end coughing and completely disoriented. The gas masks had to be carried at all times in their square cardboard boxes slung across the shoulders by a string. The boxes were always in the way. They got caught on doorknobs and jostled against people. On one occasion my box was caught in a closing underground door. I was forced against the glass by the tug of the box dangling outside the door as the train roared through the tunnel. Thereafter, I pressed the box under my arm whenever I entered or exited anywhere.

Lilka entered the Institute of Art and I signed up to read history at the university. The following day, I took my letter of recommendation from John Guinness and went by the underground to Fleet Street for an interview with Mr. Blunt, publisher and editor of *Sailplane & Glider* magazine.

He was seated behind an enormous mahogany desk, puffing his ruddy cheeks as if he were chewing. I stood before him with John's recommendation in my nervous hand while he squinted at me through horn-rimmed glasses. His mannerism was that of an old man. Actually, he was about thirty—still quite old, in my view.

"Well, give it to me." His voice blasted around me like a thunderclap. Uneasily I handed him John's letter. He placed it on his desk. "You can start right now."

I did not have the sense to ask him about hours to be worked or about pay.

Impatiently he instructed me how to do a paste-up and told me the address of the printshop, then put on his bowler hat, took his umbrella out of its stand, and left.

The magazine was Mr. Blunt's passion. It was an extension of his enthusiasm for gliding. The rest of his energy he devoted to having his wife produce a soccer team of children for him. Mrs. Blunt now had four girls and three boys. Obviously, she was going to be kept busy for many years to come.

Before I was allowed to write one word for the magazine, I had to experience gliding.

On a Saturday, Mr. Blunt drove me in his Rolls Royce to his estate in Bury St. Edmunds. He introduced me to his tired, pregnant wife. Seven children were racing through the house in undisciplined joy, while Mrs. Blunt ordered tea and scones. After Mr. Blunt sent the children out of sight, we sat in silence as we ate. Mrs. Blunt lowered her eyes and folded her hands into her lap. Before I could finish my tea, Mr. Blunt commanded me to follow him. I thanked Mrs. Blunt, who did not look up or respond. I traipsed after Mr. Blunt.

Mr. Blunt and I soared over the downs of Dover. Silently suspended between sea and sky, the turmoil of life became the stuff of insubstantial smoke. The soughing of the sea merged with air currents into an empyrean dream. We went every weekend. I loved it and dreamed of becoming a pilot. Then I would be able to float above the absurdity of the discord below.

I was now allowed to write articles about soaring, and I seldom saw Mr. Blunt. He left the magazine in my hands. I sat behind his imposing desk, enjoying my good fortune.

The office was across from the Old Bailey, and sometimes I would go into the courthouse and listen to litigations. The ridiculous wigs on serious men amused me. Some of the contests seemed absurd in an exploding world.

My daily routine included a visit to the post office across the street. I had written to Uncle Charles in New York and he had sent me a letter in which he had enclosed a guarantee that I would not be a ward of the state should I ever wish to come to the States. I had no desire to go the States, but I wrote and thanked him. Our correspondence was intermittent but detailed.

Teo's letters came sporadically. His training was completed, he was thrilled to be a fighter pilot. We spent the two weekend passes he had in passionate embraces under exploding bombs, oblivious to the world. Then he was gone. Shot down over the Straits of Dover.

Lilka and I mourned for months. Anthony was our consolation. Gaunt and tired, he took us on his weekend passes to the Polish restaurant a block away, where we ate plates of fried mushrooms—no food coupons needed—and talked about Teo's heroism.

"He died for freedom," said Anthony.

"Not for his," Lilka said. She reached for his hand. "Please don't die for mine."

I left and wandered among the ruins. It did not seem to me that his dying would change anything. I knew I would never fall in love again.

Then Anthony was shot down, and our lives caved in. There seemed to be no consolation anywhere among the ruins and death. The wailing of the air-raid sirens, the bomber formations overhead immediately after the sirens sounded, the bombings, the collapsing buildings, the gathering of the maimed and dead—these were constant reminders that life hung by a slender thread.

For more than a year we had been reading warning signs about the German secret weapon. Suddenly, it burst across the sky and landed in our lives.

One morning, walking down Oxford Street on our way to university, we spotted a small plane sputtering across the sky spitting fire from its tail.

We watched it glide above the city. Then the engine stopped and the plane began to spiral to earth in ever-smaller circles, nose down. It hit the ground some distance away, but the concussion from its explosion threw us to the ground. I covered my head with my hands to protect myself from falling stones and plaster.

"Hey, look, Lilka. The anti-aircraft crew hit a plane."

"That's one for Teo and Anthony."

"It won't bring them back."

Then we saw another little plane speed across the sky and plunge to earth in a fountain of fire.

Then they came in ever-greater numbers. We still believed these were small German planes being shot down—retribution for Teo and Anthony.

People rose from the pavement and, looking bewildered, brushed themselves off as ambulances and fire trucks rolled up Regents Street. Flames licked roofs a few blocks away and smoke rose in a sooty funnel. People ran in all directions.

The spitting planes crashed randomly, and we wondered why the blimps floating over London did not stop these German trespassers. At last, the government announced that these were rockets—the secret weapons London had been warned about.

Relieved to know what the secret weapon was, we were now afraid of not knowing where the next one would crash, and walked hunched in anticipation.

The sirens screeched continually. As more than two thousand V-1 rockets trashed the city, Londoners humorously dubbed them "Doodlebugs."

One of them struck several blocks away from my office. I sought shelter from the falling debris and flying glass under Mr. Blunt's sturdy mahogany desk just as the ceiling collapsed. Imprisoned under the desk by beams and bricks, I frantically dug through the airless rubble, choking on the dust. After more digging, I managed to crawl out of my tomb coughing and wheezing, covered with plaster.

I discovered that the office was hanging in the air. A patch of sky broke through the hole in the ceiling. Plaster sifted down in shovelfuls. I crept to the edge where the window had been and waited for air-raid wardens to rescue me.

That ended the publication of *Sailplane & Glider*. Mr. Blunt was in the country, presumably adding to his stock of soccer players, and I never saw him again.

Lilka and I augmented our income during the summers and holidays by touring England with a Czech dance troupe. Sometimes we were paid with a treat of bangers and chips at the local pubs, sometimes merely with a few flowers thrown from the audience onto the stage, and sometimes we were actually paid in cash.

London was swarming with struggling humanity from all parts of the globe. Refugees from Europe came to seek shelter. Soldiers in tunics and turbans, khaki and blue, choked the streets. Along with the daily tragedies went an aura of licentiousness. "Here today and gone tomorrow" was an attitude expressed in lethargic indifference or frenetic activity.

Yet our lives were routine. We did our ARP duty, worked, and went to classes. I learned from the study of history that, for centuries, war has been a continuous shifting and changing of borders, cultures, and displaced peoples. I read about decisive battles and about warriors whose heroism was measured by the number of enemies killed. Wars were fought for water, salt, gold, power, land, religion, and for whatever atavistic reasons men can find for fighting. What was not recorded in the history books was the heroism and misery of the people who became the victims of war. It was all so senseless and distressing.

The hostel in which we stayed was reduced to smoldering ruins in an air raid while Lilka and I were in class. So we moved, and we moved, and we moved—from place to place. We lived in pensions, hostels, dormitories, and rented rooms. After our first confident unpacking at Holborn, we did not unpack again, but lived out of our suitcase. When the windows blew out and the plaster came down, we needed only to dig it out, wander the streets, find a newspaper, and search for a room. I tried to heed my mother's words: "With common sense you can live anywhere." But common sense had nothing to do with it. Most certainly the ideologies of leaders made the choices of where I lived. Since I knew little about the comforts of home, nothing much of family togetherness and permanence, this constant wandering from one room to another did not bother me, nor would it in the future.

The sky was ablaze with exploding shells and showers of shrapnel. Searchlights knifed through the sky and crisscrossed the night. Descending flares illuminated shattered roofs and buried houses.

Though Lilka insisted on going into bomb shelters during raids, I was unable to be in such crowded places. The press of humanity felt smothering. I found it hard to breathe in a crowd so I sought shelter in doorways.

One night, I stood in an empty street and watched the bursting shells of anti-aircraft fire and the planes darting after the secret intruders. All around me the ruins expanded and converged into a merciless range of fire.

A young man in a dark blue uniform ran toward me, head down, collar up. The gold buttons on his tunic reflected the flames bursting all around him. He grabbed my arm.

"What do you think you're doing?" I pulled away.

"I was just trying to pull you to safety." His accent was French.

"I can take care of myself."

"All right," he said and ran under a doorway, the standard procedure when seeking protection from the bombings. I walked to the door and stood beside him.

"Jacques Macron," he said, his voice drowned by the sound of failing bombs.

"Miriam Darvas," I said and extended my hand.

"What a way to spend the last day of my leave," he said.

"Would you like to come to my place and meet my friend?" I said.

When the all-clear sounded, we walked through the smoldering debris and stopped to help dig victims out of the rubble. The smell of blood and the sound of screams and moans permeated the air and floated on the dust of smoldering dull gray smoke.

Lilka was sitting on the steps with our suitcase, waiting for me. The roof had caved in.

"I was worried about you," she said.

"Well, here I am and this is Jacques."

Another raid siren sounded so we ran to Hyde Park and cowered under the whistling bombs, descending like clustered fingers of death accompanied by the smell of gun smoke.

After the all-clear sounded again, Jacques left.

"Did you have to bring another flyer?" Lilka asked.

"I like him."

"It's only been a year since Teo was killed."

"A year is a long time in war, or hadn't you noticed?"

"Don't be so callous."

"I'm not callous."

"I'm not ever going to love anyone in uniform again."

"Me neither," I said. "Let's go and find someplace to live."

We bought a newspaper and started looking for digs.

We found an attic room. The roof was so frail that every tremor caused by rocket, plane, and anti-aircraft burst threatened to bring it down.

This cardboard house with the sword of Damocles hanging over it was the domain of a Polish refugee, a Mr. Rosenblum.

It was Mr. Rosenblum who reminded us that neither Lilka nor I was Jewish, because we were not born of Jewish mothers.

I finally realized what my father had tried to explain to me before we left Berlin. Religion had not been an issue in our house. Mother was a Catholic and Father was more a political activist than a Jew. But we had been labeled Jews. The thought, that my father had died as one, and that had I been captured crossing the border I might have died as a member of a group that did not accept me, was tragic. I wanted to weep.

Lilka said that regardless of what Mr. Rosenblum believed, we were in the same predicament as he was.

On the basis of our being non-Jews, Mr. Rosenblum offered us room and board in return for our doing various household duties on Fridays and Saturdays, when his wife was not permitted to work. Board consisted of kosher food, to which we contributed our ration coupons. From sunset Friday till sunset Saturday we lit the stove, turned on lights, washed dishes, and combed the hair of the Rosenblums' four daughters.

Mr. Rosenblum was a short man. His small frame was encased in baggy black pants and a loose, long, black jacket. The sleeves of his coat were so long that only his fingertips were in evidence. Long, coarse, gray-black hair protruded under the black hat he wore over his yarmulke. Sideburns hung in ringlets around his ears. His long beard was a matted mass that covered his concave chest. A pair of keen black eyes peered through this nest. A startlingly high-pitched voice pierced his full mustache and rose and fell in an unintelligible singsong as he lurched through the house.

Whenever he encountered me, his black eyes squinted. This generally meant he had something to say, usually a criticism. I squinted back at him and waited for his words to sputter forth. He had to gather them before he spoke. When he had placed them in order, he spat them out quickly as if he were afraid to lose them. Once his statement was out, he would turn abruptly, lurch to his door, kiss the small mezuzah nailed to the doorframe, and disappear into his room.

Mrs. Rosenblum, taller than her husband, was thin and angular. She was an apparition of singular absurdity as she shuffled through the house glassy-eyed and silent, her wig askew. No mirrors were allowed. She walked with her head down as if she were searching the floor for some lost item, or perhaps an infinitesimal spot of dust left by my carelessness. Her elbows were rigidly pressed against the sides of her body, her right hand cupped firmly over the fisted left one. She held this ball of hands clasped closely to her stomach, as if she were protecting herself from some intruder.

She scrubbed and polished obsessively, cleansing the house of unseen interlopers. Her four daughters, ranging in age from seven to fourteen, were uncommonly timid and slavishly submissive. They were not allowed outside the house and were instructed only in the esoteric writings of Maimonides and the Talmud.

We had made friends with Esther, the eldest Rosenblum daughter. She would climb the stairs to our room, furtively looking behind her for her mother, while we watched her progress from the slit in the door. The moment she reached the top landing, we pulled her into the room. The three of us huddled on the iron bed, the only place to sit, and took turns reading. Eventually she began to read some of the books we had lying around.

One day, we were sitting on our one single bed, taking turns reading D. H. Lawrence's *Lady Chatterley's Lover*. It was banned in England, but we had borrowed a copy from Gerald at the Cosmos Café.

Esther sat in a state of flushed excitement and lack of understanding, while Lilka and I giggled with the thrill of discovering forbidden sex. As we were about to find out what was going to happen to Lady Chatterley in the caretaker's cottage, Mrs. Rosenblum burst in.

"What's that?" she demanded in Polish, her fist firmly pressed against her stomach.

Lilka shrugged her shoulder and put the book under her

pillow. "Nothing," she said, eyes wide with innocent wonder.

Trying to disappear, Esther hunched her shoulders. Mrs. Rosenblum grabbed her by the ear and pulled her up and out the door while Esther squirmed and squealed.

At supper Mr. Rosenblum demanded the book, but we pretended we did not understand what he wanted. He labored up the stairs and returned to the table with the book.

Mr. Rosenblum's eyes narrowed to their usual slits and the arrows of words tumbled out in his high-pitched, Polish-accented English. "You haf contaminated my house. You do zat again, and you vill haf to leaf."

"Fine," Lilka snatched the book out of Mr. Rosenblum's hand and marched out of the room. I followed.

"The whole world is crazy," she said and put the book in our suitcase.

Not long after that episode, I wandered into the house eating a chocolate. Mrs. Rosenblum had emphatically explained the absolute necessity of preparing and eating the milchisch dishes separate from the fleischisch dishes on our arrival.

I reasoned that the candy bar was not a meat dish; therefore it had to be a milk dish. In any event, I ate it out of the wrapper, so it was not likely to be in contact with any dishes.

Mrs. Rosenblum shuffled toward me. She stopped suddenly. Her eyes opened wide, her mouth snapped for air, and her hand knotted tightly into her stomach.

"What's that?" Her voice had a high-pitched tremor.

I looked behind me, wondering what could cause her such distress.

She pointed at the chocolate. "What's that?" she repeated.

"This?" I extended the chocolate bar. She took two steps back and threw her hands up as if protecting herself from attack.

"It's only chocolate."

"Get out. Get out at vonz viz zat unkosher food." Her shrill cry was almost a scream.

I went outside and sat on the front stairs, thinking about sharing the chocolate episode with Lilka. The air-raid siren sounded and a second later an explosion nearby threw me to the ground and blew the chocolate right out of my hand. Showered with falling plaster and shattered glass, my heart pounded like a jackhammer.

A little while later, I saw Lilka stumbling over debris on her way toward me. She sat down on the pile of bricks surrounding me.

"Hey, it's over, you can sit up now."

I climbed out of the rubble and told her about the chocolate, with dramatic embellishments.

"My last coupon went into that candy bar," I lamented. "And now it's buried over there." I pointed to a pile of plaster in the street. We laughed until our sides hurt and dusty tears rolled down our faces.

Though the house was still standing, broken bricks and shattered glass blocked the entrance. Lilka studied the building for a moment.

"Well, let's get the suitcase and find another place."

"We've got to do our air raid post duty first."

We crunched over dust and plaster into the house. Mr. Rosenblum greeted us with a wild stare. We brushed past him. Crumbled plaster and glass shards littered the stairs. The attic window was blown out and the flames of the fires danced across the wall. We got our gas masks and helmets and climbed back down.

"You haf defiled zis house," Mr. Rosenblum called after us as we ran to our duty posts.

Twisted girders, leaning walls, piles of brick, and broken bodies lay in disarray as we arrived where the bomb had landed. Crying women leaned on piles of rubbish and screaming children lay on the ground, broken and bleeding. Arms and legs protruded from collapsed houses. After carrying the children to waiting ambulances, we dug for the bodies belonging to the buried arms or legs. Some were alive and could be resuscitated; others were too mangled to be saved. I heard a whimper. I dug frantically till I saw a small leg. I dug more. I pulled out a boy about three or four years old, gasping for breath. His legs were at odd angles and he was bleeding from his head. I took him in my arms and wiped his face. His lips were moving and I leaned over him to hear better. "Mama," he whispered and then he died. I rocked and rocked him in my arms. My tears tasted bitter. A medic tried to take the boy from me, but I could not let go of him.

"Is he yours?" he asked.

"No."

"You're lucky."

Oh, yes, I was lucky. I had a dead child in my arms who was not mine.

"He's dead, you know."

I knew, but I kept rocking the small body.

Lilka took the boy out of my arms and took him to the ambulance. All I wanted to do was to sleep in order to forget, but Lilka pulled me up and led me through the rubble.

"I don't want to go to the Rosenblums'," I said. I could not face the religious concerns about milchisch and fleis-chich when all around the world was going to hell.

"We'll have a bath and then we'll find another place."

This seemed reasonable enough and I let myself be led to the Rosenblums' house.

Lilka inserted a shilling into the hot water heater, known as the Geyser, and got a metered quarter tub of water. For economic reasons we shared the bath.

Mrs. Rosenblum came lumbering up the stairs and pounded on the bathroom door. "It is forbidden to bas in Sabbath. Get out at vons."

This edict had patently not been conceived under the conditions of modern warfare.

You are breaking our laws," she yelled in her high-pitched voice.

This roused me from my stupor. I yelled, "Shut up!"

We heard her stumble over the rubbish down the stairs.

"Let's get out of here," Lilka said when the sound of Mrs.

Rosenblum's steps had vanished.

"I'm too tired to look for digs."

"You can sleep some other time. I really can't stand this anymore. Might as well go before they throw us out."

We dressed, emptied the drawer into our communal suitcase, and blundered downstairs. Mr. Rosenblum appeared out of the ashes like Mephistopheles.

"You not vashed dishes."

"We're moving," Lilka said and stepped over the rubble.

"You vash, zen leaf."

I washed, Lilka dried.

Mrs. Rosenblum, who usually absented herself from the kitchen on Saturdays, came shuffling in.

"You vill—" Her voice trailed off.

Lilka rolled her eyes. Images of the dead boy surfaced in the dishwater and I felt an urgent need to vomit.

"Oy veh, oy veh!" Mrs. Rosenblum said to the ceiling.

I kept my face over the sink. Lilka's dishcloth stopped in midair. She looked at Mrs. Rosenblum with a hint of hostility. "What now?"

"You vashing ze milchisch dishes vis ze fleischisch."

We had contaminated the dishes by washing the ones used for meat only and the ones used for dairy only together in the same pan.

I retched into the sink. Mrs. Rosenblum hurriedly left the kitchen.

"Are you all right?" Lilka patted me on the back.

I rinsed off my face and sipped water from the faucet.

"Mr. Rosenblum, come, come." Mrs. Rosenblum's frantic call hurt my ears. My knees did not want to support me.

Mr. Rosenblum lurched through the kitchen door, his wife trailing behind him. His keen eyes rolled from me to Lilka.

"Jou vill bury ze dishes in ze garten," he said in a surprisingly controlled voice.

In order to decontaminate the dishes they had to be buried in soil for three days.

The shovel shook in my hands. I dug little holes to put the dishes in and then covered them up again. The knives and forks had to be stuck in the soil too. I kept thinking of the bodies I had loaded on stretchers.

"How can they have us bury dishes when we just finished digging up dead people?" I asked Lilka.

Her foot on the shovel, Lilka said, "Nuts."

Mr. Rosenblum approached the fresh mounds of dirt and mumbled a prayer over them, turned abruptly, and glowered at us.

"You vill haf to moof."

Without a word of good-bye, we headed directly to the Cosmos Café.

The Cosmos was wedged between a pastry shop and a bookstore in a dim alley in Soho. The entry was a narrow recessed door. One had to be among the initiated to know it was there. A dark hall, filled with the aroma of baking, led to a flight of stairs illuminated by a dim yellow bulb. At the top of the stairs, cigarette smoke drifted through an open door onto the landing. Through the door was a Café, where drippy candles set into old Chianti bottles stood on tables covered with blue-and-white checkered tablecloths. Two wicker lamps were suspended by black chains from the ceiling.

Lilka had found a new love, Vaclav, a Czech flyer. He and Jacques would meet us at Cosmos.

"You said you were never going to fall in love with a flyer," I said.

"Love is unpredictable. Besides, look at you and Jacques."

"It's not permanent."

"Neither is Vaclav. Anyway, never is a long time."

I had found a job at *Lancelot*, a magazine devoted to poetry and short stories. Since our rented rooms never had a table and usually only one chair, I would go to the Cosmos to work. I would sit at the corner table by the window with my beat-up old typewriter, pencils, and paper fanned out in front of me, and would stare into the dimly lit alley, groping for words.

The patrons, mostly foreign students and artists, sat around discussing weighty subjects such as war and poetry.

One of the regulars was Gerald, the one who lent us *Lady Chatterley's Lover*. Gerald wore his hair down to his frayed shirt collar and sported a Lenin beard. His energetic convictions contrasted with his watery blue eyes. He came Fridays punctually at four o'clock, wound his way among the tables, and passed out blue mimeographed sheets of exhortations: "Workers of the world unite against your capitalist oppressors!" or "Down with capitalist imperialist wars!"

When he had littered the tables with his papers, which no one read, he sat with Lilka and me to expound his theory of world revolution. Invariably we got into an argument.

"And then the world will speak with only one voice, the voice of Communism," he said.

"One-sixth of the earth already speaks with the voice of Communism," I pointed out to him.

"That's the point. Only a sixth."

"Do you really believe that Communism will be any different from Nazism?" Lilka asked.

"Communism is a benefit to humanity, Nazism a detriment. Only the shedding of the blood of the imperialist capitalist exploiters will free the world."

"The shedding of blood is easily done over a cup of coffee," Lilka said, her elbows on the table, her chin resting in her hands.

"Stop blowing up the world, Gerald. It's being done quite efficiently without a revolution," I said.

"You simply don't understand the issues," Gerald said in his clipped, condescending English.

"Can't stand a woman disagreeing with you?" Lilka asked.

"Women are not leaders."

"There were many women in history who were leaders and are today. As for war, you men make them, you fight them," I said.

Gerald shook his head. "Typical."

"Typical," I replied. We laughed and parted.

A few days later, Gerald was killed in an air raid. As with many people who passed through my life, I never learned his surname.

My job with *Lancelot* disappeared when the building vanished in the smoke of an explosion. I got a job at the Czech embassy-in-exile and worked there as an assistant to the consul while I continued going to the university. Lilka got a job with the Czech Red Cross.

Life continued under the shadow of destruction. Food got harder to come by. We found an apartment off Knightsbridge on the second floor of an old Victorian. The windowpanes were covered with crosses of tape. It had one tiny bedroom, one small sitting room and a bath. The kitchen was a cabinet in an alcove. On top of the cabinet was an electric burner plugged into an outlet in the hall. In the cabinet were five assorted plates, three chipped cups, three forks, one knife, and a cooking pot. We used the pot to boil water for tea and to cook our one allotted egg per month.

We would sit cross-legged on the floor, the eggs carefully in front of us, and discuss earnestly how to cook the eggs—soft boiled, fried, or scrambled. The cooking of the eggs fell to Lilka since I had no inkling how to begin to break an egg.

Whenever the tenants above us moved around, plaster drifted from the ceiling to settle in uneven chunks on floor, sofa, and bed. We had to clean everything before we could go to sleep at night. Lilka slept in the sitting room on the sofa, and I had the cot in the cioset/bedroom. The lone gas heater in the sitting room had the familiar shilling deposit box locked with a bicycle lock.

The sitting room was somewhat larger than the bedroom, though it could barely accommodate the sofa, but it was ours for the time being at least.

Lilka and Vaclav talked of marriage. I was madly in love with Jacques, but avoided talk of marriage.

I had not seen Nora since we were children in Prague. We had kept in touch with sporadic correspondence. Her letters usually consisted of three sentences: How are you? I am fine. My new address is so and so.

One day, my bell rang. I did not know who this slim, shy, dark-haired girl was who stood at the threshold when I opened the door.

"Who are you looking for?" I said.

"Miriam."

"I'm Miriam."

"I'm Nora."

We stared at each other. I could not believe that this stranger was the little girl I had left behind in Prague. I had been twelve, Nora ten when I left Prague. I was now eighteen.

She explained that the school she had been in had closed, and she had nowhere to go. I gave up my closet cot for her, and slept on the sitting room floor.

Soon Nora also met a Czech flyer, another Vaclav, and the apartment was in constant motion from the coming and going of the two Vaclavs and one Jacques.

The city was in turmoil. The war seesawed. It was coming to a close, then it wasn't. Battle of the Bulge headlines loomed large in the newspapers.

Then the war was over. Jammed into Piccadilly Circus, people swayed to songs and whoops, climbed lampposts, and sat on the boarded-over statue of Eros.

The tickertape at the Czech Red Cross was ticking day and night. The names of the dead and the survivors of the concentration camps were coming in from Europe by the thousands. It was Lilka's job to read off the names of the liberated and the terminated inmates of the concentration camps. She stood on the balcony above the masses pressed into the hall below. In response to her announcements, voices of grief rose into the cupola like a wailing wind, shattering her composure.

Every day I asked about Mother and every day Lilka said that there was no news. After work we usually met at the Polish restaurant for our dinner of fried mushrooms.

One evening Lilka seemed unable to eat. She began a sentence, then stopped. I leaned over, wanting to urge her to say whatever was bothering her, but an inner voice stopped me.

She started to cry, and I knew I did not want to hear what she wanted to say to me. She put down her fork and stared at her plate. "My mother died in Theresienstadt," she whispered. The blood drained from her face.

"What?" Through the mist of my hope I wanted to console Lilka. "Theresienstadt was not an extermination camp," I said.

"If it was not an extermination camp, why did she die?"

Not knowing what to say, I contemplated my plate. Lilka leaned across the table and touched my hand. "Your mother's name is also on the list of the dead."

"Theresienstadt?"

"It's not known where."

"If it's not known where, then there might be a mistake." I clung to the idea of a mistake.

"That's a possibility," Lilka said without conviction.

Suddenly, the dream of seeing my mother again was dead. I longed hopelessly to be with my family again. Wild thoughts raced through my head.

The familiar pain of loneliness gripped me. I rushed into the street and walked aimlessly into the darkness, completely unaware of my surroundings. I felt disconsolate with my inability to save my mother and defeated by my inability to control my own fate. Rage infected me like a poison injected into my veins, wounding my spirit, making me sick. I wanted to kill all the Obermeiers of the world. Amidst the destruction of the city lay the ruins of my life. I resolved again never to be tossed about like a leaf in the wind.

This determined, I walked back to the apartment. Nora and Lilka were despondent, in tears. I felt removed, opaque.

Anger had become my permanent partner. It had wound itself around my bones and it exploded when the Czech government announced that Czechs had to return to Czechoslovakia. No edict was going to chase me again. I was not going to return to Prague regardless of the Czech government's orders.

Lilka and Nora had decided to return.

"Haven't you had enough of being forced to run?" I said.

"It's not the same as being chased."

"To me it is."

"Don't you want to go?" Lilka said.

"I'm never again going to be forced to go anywhere I don't want to go, remember?" I said.

"I can't understand you. That's your home," Lilka said.

"I have no home there or anywhere. There is nothing left for me in Prague."

"Well, I'm going," Lilka said.

"Me, too," Nora said.

"After being forced to wander all over Europe to get out of there, you want to return?"

"There goes indomitable Miriam again, going off in the opposite direction from anyone else," Lilka said.

"I'm not indomitable. I'm furious."

"You're going to have to go back. The embassy insists on it," Lilka said.

"The embassy can insist all it wants."

"What about Jacques?" Nora said.

"I'll think about that later."

"What are you going to do?" Nora said.

"You two go to Prague and I'll send you a postcard from wherever I'll be."

The postcard came from Berlin. The day before that discussion I had seen an advertisement in the newspaper placed there by the U.S. Army: "German interpreters needed. Three languages required. Apply at 500 Oxford Street." I went the next morning.

The office consisted of one desk, two chairs, and a gray-haired American sergeant by the name of Major, three stripes on his sleeve. He turned away from the window as I walked in the room.

"I'm applying for the interpreter job."

"Do you know what the job consists of?"

"Interpreting, I assume."

"If you're accepted, you will be going to Berlin."

"Fine."

"Do you realize that Berlin is destroyed?"

"So is London."

"There's no water, no electricity, no heat. The Germans are starving. You sure you want to go?"

"Sure. Berlin couldn't be any worse than London."

He pushed the newspapers cluttering his desk aside, clasped his hands in front of him, and raised an eyebrow. "You ain't seen nothing yet, kid."

I did not want to seem inexperienced in the ways of war.

"I've dug bodies from rubble."

"Hmm." He rose and walked to the window. With his back to me he asked. "Do you speak three languages?"

"If you press me I can squeeze out four."

He turned to me, his face sour, and said, "Very funny." Then he picked up the newspaper and threw it at me.

"Translate the first paragraph into German."

I took the paper and translated.

"What's the other language you know?"

"I can translate this into Czech and French."

"Go ahead."

I had the distinct impression that I could have claimed to be translating the article into Arabic and he would not have known the difference.

He clasped his hands behind his back and rocked back and forth in his chair. "Well, you're hired. First one."

"When do I leave?"

"In two weeks."

"Mr. Major –"

"Sergeant, please."

"Mr. Sergeant…" He smiled a crooked smile but let me continue.

"I have to leave within a week."

"What's the matter, you in trouble?"

"I work for the Czech embassy and they insist that I return to Prague."

I could see that I had his sympathy. His brows furrowed. "You don't want to return?"

"There's nothing to return to."

He looked at the papers on his desk, then at me as if he were considering something. I rolled and unrolled the newspaper and waited.

"So, you want out of here?"

"Yes, otherwise I will be forced to return to Prague. I have to leave."

"There's a plane leaving in three days. Think you can make it?"

I felt like embracing him but smiled instead. "Sure, I can make it." I would have made it if he had told me the plane was leaving in an hour.

"Go to this tailor in Regents Street with this note. He can make your uniform in twenty-four hours. He knows the kind of uniforms we want." He handed me the note. "Come back when you have the uniform and I'll issue your orders."

I raced down Regents Street to the tailor.

Two days later I reported back to Sergeant Major in my new uniform.

"Looks great. First time I've seen it on anyone. Turn around."

I turned to show him my new outfit, pleased with myself.

"Here are your orders. You're taking a military transport. Plane leaves at midnight."

I took the papers, unable to believe that I was actually leaving England on my own terms.

He put his hand on my shoulder and led me to the door, opened it, and slapped me on the back.

"Well, good luck with all them GIs."

We shook hands and I left.

I entered the apartment in my battle dress. Both Vaclavs were there. Lilka and Nora were packing, and the two Vaclavs were making suggestions as to what to take and what to leave behind. Jacques was helping as well.

"My God, what's that?" Lilka said when she saw me enter.

"I like it," Jacques said.

"I'm leaving for Germany tomorrow."

Both Vaclavs looked at me as if I had gone mad. Nora's Vaclav said, "How can you go to Germany?"

"By plane."

"You know damn well what I mean."

"You explain it to me."

Lilka's Vaclav took over with a lecture about going to the land of my enemies, and Nora said, "How could you?"

"I'm going with the occupation troops. More like conquering the enemy than going back to the enemy. That's revenge."

"What kind of revenge is that? You can't kill them," Vaclav said.

"It's better than none."

"Come with us," Lilka said.

"There's nothing left for me in Prague. I'd be reminded of everything that I lost."

"Do what you must," Lilka said and hugged me.

We parted. Every separation for me was a final one. I knew nothing of temporary absences.

Jacques and I left them amid protestations and accusations. We went to the Polish restaurant for a plate of fried mushrooms and Polish bread. We held hands across the table.

"What about us?" Jacques said.

"I don't know."

He sank into an abject silence, and I did not know what more to say.

We left the restaurant arm in arm. The waiter wished me good luck.

For a while we walked the streets of London aimlessly till we came to Hyde Park. Only a few lamps lit the park. No searchlights crisscrossed the sky. A few blimps were still tethered to the ground, the last vestiges of London's defense system.

We sat down under a tree.

"Let's get married, too," Jacques said.

"I don't know."

"Please marry me," he said.

I resisted. "I want to, but I can't," I said.

"What kind of silly answer is that?"

I knew in the marrow of my bones that whomever I attached myself to would be destroyed by a bomb, snatched from me by a sudden turn of political events, or lost in a turmoil of escaping humanity. The fear of loss was in my viscera like a burning coal. Kurt, Mother, Father, Steffie, Lex, Chris, Angelika, and Teo: each a red grit of pain lodged in my circulating blood. I wanted to be free of the pain of loss by making no permanent attachments.

"You have no address, I have no address. We can't even keep in touch," I said.

"Here's my uncle's old address, though I doubt that it still exists." He scribbled a Paris address on the inside of a matchbook cover and handed it to me. I put it into my pocket.

"You sure you won't change your mind and come with me to France?" His voice was liquid with pain.

I did not answer. My mind was in turmoil. I did so want to be with Jacques, but my fear of losing him was more powerful than my desire for him.

We sat in silence, each engrossed in painful thoughts. For years I had missed belonging and now I was rejecting it.

At the airfield we embraced on the tarmac and for one brief moment I wanted to stay. The propellers whirred, GIs were loading, and the anxiety and thrill of the unknown tugged at me. I disengaged myself from Jacques's embrace and walked to the plane. On the steps I turned. Jacques stood with his hands in his trouser pockets. I waved. He did not move. I did not know why I felt guilty. Knowing would not have changed anything that went before, yet leaving him was lacerating.

As the plane shuddered into its climb, I knew I would not see Jacques again, and a dizzying rush of panic engulfed me. The gray waters of the Channel below and the gray clouds through which we flew reinforced my sense of loss.

1945

Back to Berlin

I was on my way to Germany as a member of the Allied Expeditionary Forces, a civilian employee of the conquering army, officially known as an ACE, Allied Civilian Employee, with the pay of first lieutenant. What riches. A blue triangular patch on my right khaki sleeve announced "Censorship USA." I pictured myself as the avenger of all the wrongs these Germans had done.

My cap was wedged into the left epaulet of my battle dress jacket, my beige tie knotted into a neat Windsor knot—thanks to Miss Winton's persistence at Brighton & Hove. I anticipated high adventure, and yet I was apprehensive. This was the city where my traumas began. This was where Kurt was beaten to death. This was the town that had made me a stateless person, a refugee belonging nowhere. Was I demented, going to the city where my nightmares had begun? Still I had a sense of revenge. I was returning with the occupation forces, the mighty conquerors.

We were sitting in a C-47, a veteran of many sorties. A shrapnel hole had been plugged with a huge cork, the painting of Betty Grable had faded, and the seats along its body had been polished over the years by apprehensive troops being flown to dangerous destinations. The twenty-two-year-old pilot flew with the confidence of a veteran, and he was bringing us into Berlin's Tempelhof Airport through a dense fog.

The landing strip was invisible and as the plane descended the right wing hit a radio tower. The sudden collision blew the cork across the aisle. The force of the impact threw all ten soldiers into a pile. The plane bounced over potholes and debris, tipped sideways, and came to a stop.

A colonel rose, brushed himself off, and gave me a hand. We listed toward the blown door and jumped to the tarmac. The rest of the passengers followed.

Surrounding the airport was a pile of rubble blocking the view of the city.

"Where's the exit from this mess?" the colonel asked no one in particular.

The pilot jumped out of the cabin. "You gotta climb over it. Someone will be on the other side with a truck." He led the pack of stragglers to the mountain of rubble and began to climb on all fours. We followed, slipping and sliding over smoky dust and rolling debris. On the other side of this pile of refuse was the view of what was left of the city. Scattered bricks and concrete, perilously tilting walls and grotesquely twisted girders lined a cleared path. A military truck was the only intact object in sight. We piled in.

Watching the dead city glide by, I had to admit that the sergeant was right: I ain't seen nothing yet.

Uprooted trees, burnt and leafless, lay strewn about. Half-destroyed houses, black with soot, cowered in the debris. Their jagged hollow walls crept out of the ruins like burnt fingers reaching for life. People scurried over piles of debris and disappeared in holes and crevices. Children with dirty faces and ragged clothing scampered barefoot among the ruins, scavenging for food and cigarette butts. Whatever food they could scrounge they carried home in tin cans tied around their necks. These hungry and frightened people had chased me from one country to another and even followed me with their bombs. Could these people have been the dreaded Ubermenschen? Though I could not forgive them, the rage that had eaten my bones was a little diffused by these poor, hungry, gray figures stumbling over the ruins. Still, I hoped that Obermeier and Otto were among the wrecks.

I wondered what exactly the war had accomplished. Men had fought great battles: the Battle of the Bulge, the battle for Monte Casino, the battle for the beaches, for God and country, for God and freedom, for God and a pure race. They had left hundreds of cities in ruins and their people without shelter or food. Whose side had God been on? God, I supposed, was on the victors' side. Who was free? Only the dead.

The truck stopped in front of a building stenciled with bullet holes, windows boarded. The truck driver, a young GI, came around the back.

"You and the colonel are assigned here for the night. You…" he pointed at me, "report to your commanding officer tomorrow." He helped me jump off the truck.

"How do I get to him?"

"Use your thumb," he snapped over his shoulder and jumped into the driver's seat.

Women were clearing the bricks and debris into wheelbarrows and old men carted them off. I had imagined these people as the mighty of the world, these poor, bedraggled creatures. They were, after all, only human, and in their suffering they were equal to their victims.

As darkness descended, the figures vanished into the ruins. There was an eerie silence. No sound of streetcars clanking, no birds singing or dogs barking.

The young colonel nudged me. "We hit the jackpot."

"What does that mean?"

"Look."

A sign across the entrance of the building proclaimed our overnight accommodations to be the "Los Angeles Hotel." It was a great house once owned by a Jewish family. It was taken from them by the by the Nazis, but now it was requisitioned by the Americans for overnight stays by incoming American military personnel.

We pushed through the entrance and were enclosed by darkness.

A voice cut through the dark. "Over here, sir."

A soldier motioned us to a desk that was lit by the flicker of a candle. He lit two candles and handed one to me and one to the colonel.

"Follow me."

We stumbled up a wide, winding staircase. On the first landing, the soldier opened a door into a room with a bed and a nightstand.

"This is yours." He held the door open for me. "There's some water in a pitcher in the corner for washing. Don't drink it. Toilet's across the hall, bucket of water is for flushing."

He closed the door and I was left with the candle casting ghostly shadows.

Visible through the slits of the boards on the window, monstrous ruins rose like ghosts from unlit streets. I placed the candle on the nightstand and sat on the bed wondering whether I should have taken the sergeant who hired me in London more seriously.

I took off my shoes and crawled fully clothed into bed.

Something awakened me during the night. The candle flickered. It was about to go out in the last spatter of wax and wick when in its small circle of light a rat appeared. It sat at the corner of the nightstand observing me with eyes like glowing coals. I covered my head with the scratchy army blanket and hoped it would go away.

I was awakened by light seeping through the wooden window slits and strips of light crawling under the door. At last someone knocked.

"Coffee and toast," a voice announced. I bounced out of bed and flung open the door. A soldier walked into the room carrying a tray.

"There's a rat in my room. Right there." I pointed to an empty nightstand.

"They're all over." He shrugged and placed the tray on the nightstand right where the rat had sat.

"Can I eat this somewhere else?"

"On the stairs, if you like."

I followed him out the door with tray in hand, reluctant to be left alone in this mausoleum with rats everywhere. "Where's the coffee and toast from?"

"We bring it from the mess."

He descended the winding stairs.

"How do I get to my commanding officer?" I said to his back.

Aware that I was trying to delay his departure, he came back up the stairs. "Who is he?" he asked, and sat down beside me.

"Colonel Leahy."

"I can take you there. I'm going off duty in twenty minutes."

He talked while I ate. He was anxious to go home to the States. He had enough points, but the bottleneck in Bremerhaven delayed his departure.

"How long are you here for?" he asked.

"Two years."

"Sure hope you can stand this pit." He rose. "See you shortly," he said, and disappeared around the bend of the stairs.

I walked to the pitcher of water, keeping a lookout for rats, splashed my face, and then went to the toilet. The situation looked more promising when I discovered a roll of toilet paper there.

Halfway down the stairs I met the soldier and the colonel. We drove to headquarters.

The streets were cleared of rubble in narrow ribbons. We bounced over rocks and potholes down a street devoid of life. No houses lined the street, only here and there a burnt frame was close to toppling. Compared to London, Berlin was in total ruin. The Allies had done their job well.

The soldier dropped me off at HQ and drove off with the colonel.

A brass plate on a door in a corridor bustling with activity announced "Col. G. Leahy, USMG." I learned that USMG meant U.S. Military Government.

I knocked and entered. Colonel Leahy was a man of about fifty with a weathered, ruddy complexion that looked bright red against his white mustache. His gray hair was cropped in the military style and stood up on his head like stiff bristles. Under his white eyebrows were galvanic blue eyes.

The war had been over for a month, but Colonel Leahy still treated soldiers as if they were troops under fire and made no exception with me.

He looked up. "You, I suppose, are the new *ACE*?" I thought I heard him swallow a "ha" at the end of the sentence. He opened my 201 file, leafed through it, and then closed it. "You Darvas?"

"Yes."

Suddenly, he slapped his right hand on the desk and jumped up. "You're a wall!"

I stepped back. "I'm a wall?"

With both hands on the desk now, he leaned forward. His blue eyes glittered. "AWOL, as in A-W-O-L."

"I don't know that word."

He sat down emphatically, placed his elbows on the desk, and put his head in his hands. Not knowing exactly what to do, I remained standing, waiting for another outburst.

He raised his head and squinted at me. "It means away without leave. You were supposed to be here five days ago. Where were you?"

"Paris."

"Paris. What the hell were you in Paris for?"

"The plane landed there."

"What do you mean the plane landed there?"

"The plane landed there for a few hours and I wanted to see Paris again. The pilot said there's a daily shuttle for Berlin so I took a few days off."

Actually, I had gone to the address Jacques had given me. It was an effort to assuage my guilt about leaving him. Jacques was right. Like many people in those days, his uncle had disappeared without a trace. I wanted to keep in contact with Jacques, in the vague belief that I might get over my fear of losing everyone I cared for and marry him after all. The possibility was gone. For a fleeting moment I wondered whether I should have married him. Colonel Leahy continued. "You can't take days off when you haven't worked, and you can't take off without the express permission of your commanding officer, which is me."

"You weren't there."

"We have a joker among us now. And an *ACE* at that."

The word "ACE" sounded like an expletive. Since I had no reply to that, I stood before him and waited. The conversation took an unexpected turn.

"You know how to set up a censorship station?" His white eyebrows lifted, wrinkling his forehead.

"I'm here as an interpreter."

"I don't give a shit what you're here for, we need someone to set up a censorship station."

Summoning up boldness, I said rashly, "Just give me a desk, a telephone, and two assistants who know what they're doing."

"Done. In future, when you want to go to Paris you will request a TDY."

"TDY?"

Leahy released a sigh and rolled his eyes. "Temporary Duty."

"I will."

"I will, sir."

"Excuse me?"

"You will address me as sir."

"Of course."

"Sir. Of course, sir."

"Sir."

"That's better."

He shook his head and rolled his eyes, then cranked the field telephone. "Get Tech Sergeant Olsen and Private Biaggi here on the double."

The hall still echoed with their gallop when they came through the door, stood at attention, and saluted. Leahy returned the salute by touching his head. He pointed at the sergeant, then at the private.

"This is Tech Sergeant Olsen and PFC Biaggi."

"And this is Darvas, in charge of censorship. You help her set it up," Leahy said it as if it pained him.

A groan escaped from Biaggi.

"Jesus, sir, you saddle me with this and I'll never get home," said Olsen.

Col. Leahy grinned, exposing a row of tobacco-stained teeth. "Any more bitching from you guys and I'll assign you to her permanently. Report tomorrow morning at 0600." He waved his hand in a 'get out' gesture.

Olsen and Biaggi looked me over critically once we were in the hall. Mario Biaggi had classic Italian good looks. Everything from his curly dark hair to his brown eyes and olive skin was put together to perfection. He carried a chip on the shoulders of his stocky five-ten frame. His buddies called him Tiny.

George Olsen was tall, slender, blond, and blue-eyed, the Nordic opposite of Biaggi. He seldom got excited, but had a slow smoldering streak of anger in him. His nickname was Spike.

Both men had been in the trenches, were eager to go home, and were not at all enthusiastic about having to work in Berlin. Tiny Biaggi, the mail clerk, said to Spike Olsen, the tech sergeant, under his breath, "Jesus Christ, a girl in charge!"

Spike pretended he had not heard.

"I don't know anything about censorship," Tiny said glowering at me.

"Well, I don't either. You're the mail clerk, maybe you'll come up with some ideas."

"I won't."

Tiny and Spike promised to pick me up the next morning so that I would not have to hitchhike.

The following morning we drove to HQ through the moonscape of destruction.

Colonel Leahy greeted me. "I got an order here for you to go to Frankfurt headquarters and start a censorship station there first. So get your ass there."

"My donkey, sir?"

"Jesus. You better learn American fast. Get your behind on a plane today and take Biaggi and Olsen with you. Here's a TDY.

I took the orders and marched out. I left it up to Tiny and Spike to find a way to Frankfurt and by afternoon we were on a C-47.

After landing in Frankfurt, we climbed over more rubble. The only way to get around was by hitching rides on military trucks, command cars, and jeeps. We got a ride to headquarters in a jeep. Headquarters was in the I.G. Farben building, which bustled with the energy of uniformed men organizing the government of a destroyed country. Orders and edicts flew in all directions about prisoners of war, concentration camp inmates, displaced persons, and natives. New laws and rules for the conquered Germans were implemented and the hunt for Nazis was on. One way to capture them was through the mails, and setting up censorship had fallen to Tiny, Spike, and me.

Tiny and Spike were assigned to some German barracks, and I was billeted in a house in Frauenstein Platz, with the German owner living in the basement.

The following day we reported to a Colonel Fitzsimmons. He swiveled around in his chair to greet us with his swagger stick pointing at me. "No leave, no TDY, no days off till you've got this thing working. Understood?"

"Understood, sir."

Tiny actually knew more than he was willing to admit. Since he preferred to live in Berlin rather than Frankfurt, he spat out information as fast as he could so that he could return to Berlin. Spike set up a rotating address card file filled with names and addresses of suspects given to us by the Information and Records group in our G-2 Division. We worked from June until September nonstop. By August, the *ACEs* were pouring in from Belgium, France, England, and Holland to man the file cards.

Sacks of mail were dumped on the floor. Women ACEs compared names and addresses on the letter to the names of suspected Nazis on the card racks. If a name on the letter matched the name on the list, it was sent to Information and Records where it was analyzed and then handed to MPs for arrest.

Tiny, Spike, and I wandered at night from club to club set up for the entertainment of the conquering heroes. Mornings we dragged ourselves to work.

In September we flew back to Berlin and reported to Colonel Leahy.

"I understand you did a good job," he said blowing his cigar smoke to the ceiling. "Go find her some quarters."

I looked at him quizzically.

"Housing," he explained. He shook his head. "Where did they find you?"

"You know sir. England."

"I suppose they must know what they're doing."

"I understand that it was impossible to find Americans who spoke three languages fluently, sir."

"You speak three languages? English, I gather, isn't one of them."

"American English isn't, sir."

"What do we need three languages for? Let 'em learn English." He waved his "get out" gesture. "Dismissed."

With Colonel Leahy's permission, we drove in his command car south on Potsdammer Chaussee to the suburb of Dahlem. Houses still standing there could be requisitioned, and I could choose which one I wanted. I picked one with a garden and a picket fence. Requisitioned houses had electricity, water, and heat allocated to them. I did not have the heart to evict the owners, the Ruperts, and permitted them to stay as servants. Though they did not much like being occupied, it was better than dying of cold and hunger. I was suspicious of them. They bowed and made explanations about not knowing what had happened. I wanted to shout at them: "Didn't you smell the burning flesh? Didn't you see the cattle cars with the thin arms of their cargo waving through the slits? Didn't you hear the cries?" Instead, I insisted they live in the basement. It was still not punishment enough for them, I felt. They did get electricity, hot water, and food, which were denied most Germans who had no home left. I felt for their twelve-year-old daughter, Margot. War, hunger, and fear had scarred her—as it had me. Her arms were mere bones, her face was thin and pale, and her brown eyes were always moist, as if she were trying to prevent her tears from bursting down her cheeks. I remember my mother worrying about my thin, pale face. I brought Margot clothes and books and candies and sometimes took her with me to the theater. I could not bring myself to be civil to her parents.

The houses were separated by large gardens, and though the gardens were unkempt, the street had a dreamlike quality. It sat surrounded by destruction like a film set sprung to life under the direction of a set designer. Nothing looked familiar. The trees I remembered were gone, the houses in ruins. I could not remember the name of the street where I had lived or where it had been. It might have been in what they now called the Russian Sector, the French Sector, or the English Sector. I did not know. I was relieved there was nothing to remind me of Kurt and my home. Yet sadness hung over me like a suffocating smoke.

Berlin was an open city. It was hedonistic and schizophrenic. The Russians, French, English, and Americans passed from sector to sector without restrictions. In the American sector any cellar, house, or club that was not destroyed was requisitioned and turned into a nightclub, a bar, or a theater.

While the Berliners cowered in their bombed-out cellars, there were other cellars filled with the blaring sounds of innumerable little bands. The clubs had names like the White Helmet Club, the Forty-Eight Club, the Diablo, the Harnack House, the Titania Palast, and the Femina Club. Eating places, dancing places, and drinking places catered to the heroes who had left behind their foxholes and tanks. Wiggling females in skimpy clothes gyrated to German imitation jazz for packs of cigarettes or cans of soup. Each morning I walked through the ruins to the officers' mess followed by haggard, dirty faces of the children begging for cigarettes and scraps of food. And each morning the sound of "Oh what a beautiful morning" from the musical *Oklahoma*—played by a German band, hired for a pack of cigarettes a day—wafted across the ruins. Inside the mess were tables, set with white linen, silver, glass, and china, laden with the most delectable foods baked and cooked by German cooks, who were permitted to take the leftovers home.

During the heat of the day, the miasma of Berlin's ruins gave off a vapor that covered the city with the stench of death.

Old men and women, tied to carts like donkeys, dragged their possessions listlessly through the dusty streets. Money was worthless. American cigarettes were currency and everyone, French, English, Germans, and Russians wanted them. One carton of any American cigarette brought two-hundred dollars on the black market. Americans sold them by the thousands, converting the black market marks to dollars at the crowded exchange windows.

Cigarettes bought diamonds, pearls, gold, silver, cameras, Meissen and Rosenthal china, servants, massages, cars—anything. We wondered who got to smoke them after all the trading. Probably the farmers.

The Russians wandered around the American sector in search of fountain pens and watches. They would demand to race any German whose bicycle seemed faster than the one they had just confiscated. The Germans learned to let the Russians win the race. It became a standing joke.

Going from one sector to another merely required crossing a street. The MPs at Checkpoint Charlie waved to people coming and going. A large sign stated: "You Are Now Leaving the American Sector." Since the most frenetic activity was in the American sector, not many left to visit the other sectors.

Colonel Leahy had accepted my limited knowledge of American idioms and had even been willing to learn a few German words. "I need it on occasion," he had explained to me.

"Yeah, he needs it for his German girlfriend," Tiny said with disdain.

"Don't give me that shit," Spike said. "You've got one yourself."

"No, I ain't. She's Belgian."

"So. What's the diff?"

"If you don't know, I sure as hell can't explain it to you."

We were sitting on the steps of the office, watching the men and women cleaning the streets.

"When I get back to the States, I'm not going back to Minnesota," Spike said.

"Where you going?" Tiny asked.

"I'm going to UC Berkeley on the GI Bill."

"Where's that?" I asked.

"It's in California" Spike said. "Best school in the U.S.A."

I knew California. "Where the oranges grow as big as soccer balls?"

"Yeah, and more," Tiny said.

"Can anybody go?" I asked.

"Well, I don't know. You being a foreigner and all."

"I know she can go if someone sponsors her," Tiny said.

"In that case, maybe I'll go to Berkeley," I said.

"Who's going to sponsor you?" Tiny asked.

"You want to sponsor me?"

"You've got to have money for that. I don't have any."

"Come on, Tiny, you made as much money on the black market as anybody," Spike said.

"So did you."

"I'll sponsor you," Spike said impulsively.

"That's very nice of you, but I have a sponsor."

Spike grunted. "Some sugar daddy?"

"I have an uncle in New York. Well, he is not really my uncle, but he has already given me a 'To Whom It May Concern' paper."

"Well, here's my address anyway," Spike said and scribbled his address on a piece of paper and handed it to me. I crumpled it into my pocket.

"Here comes a Ruskie." Tiny jerked his head in the direction of an approaching lieutenant.

We watched amused as he wove toward us.

"Zdravstvui," he said and waved a wobbly arm.

"What's he saying?" Spike's eyes narrowed.

Tiny, who took offense at questions he could not answer, turned on Spike. "How the hell should I know?"

"I didn't ask you."

"Who then?"

"Miriam, of course."

"I don't speak Russian," I said.

"Well, you said Russian is a Slavic language and so is Czech."

"Sort of."

The Russian was standing before me.

"Zdravstvui," I replied.

"Ah, govoritye po Rusky."

"Ne, mluvim Cesky."

We had now clarified that I didn't speak Russian but I did Czech. Though Czech and Russian are similar in some words, inflection and sentence structure are different.

It became clear after a few minutes of negotiating between Russian and Czech that he wanted to talk to the commanding officer.

Tiny nudged me in the ribs. "What's he want?"

"I think he wants to see Leahy," I said.

"That ought to be fun." Spike grinned.

I indicated to the Russian to follow us and walked to Leahy's office.

"What the hell have you dragged in?" Leahy exploded.

"He wants to talk you," I said.

Leahy rose and was about to say something when the Russian gave a sharp salute and stood at attention. Leahy returned the salute in his usual limp noodle manner and turned to me. "You haven't answered my question."

"What question, sir?"

"What's he want?"

"I don't know, sir."

"Well, ask him!"

I mouthed the Czech words slowly as if I were talking to a deaf person and asked what it was he wanted. In slow motion he indicated a circle and said something about a clock and started to unbutton his tunic. Perplexed, we watched. Leahy's blood pressure was rising.

"Get the MPs," he said.

"Wait, wait. He wants us to do something for him, sir," I said, hoping Leahy would give the Russian a chance to explain.

The Russian exposed his arms. Wristwatches covered both from wrist to elbows.

"What the hell?" Leahy blurted. Tiny and Spike opened their mouths.

With my Czech and the Russian's response with gestures and a few Russian words, I could finally explain to Leahy that the Russian said that he had heard about the "American know-how" and wondered could one of the Americans make him a large clock out of all the wrist-watches he had collected.

Leahy's ruddy complexion became redder, his blue eyes narrowed. Anticipating an outburst of anger, I stepped behind Tiny and Spike, who were heading for the door. Suddenly a blast of guffaws rolled around the room.

Leahy pounded the desk with both his hands, his face quite purple from the strain of his roaring laughter. He gulped for air and finally sat down in his chair. He leaned his head back and laughed at the ceiling.

The Russian's brows knitted.

"I think you hurt his feelings," I said to Leahy.

"Tough shit. Get him out of here, for Chrissake, before I have the MPs throw him out." Tiny and Spike sped out the door. I pulled the Russian into the hall.

"Let's take him to the Femina Club," I suggested.

"You take him," Spike said and walked off. Tiny followed.

Though the Russians were still our allies, suspicion of them made most Americans keep their distance.

We introduced ourselves. Fyodor was his name. We wandered downtown through the darkening streets to the

Femina, where anything could be traded. We were not allowed to fraternize with the Germans, and the Femina was a German nightclub and thus was off limits. And because of that, it had become a place were the armies of all four sectors met and took their chances with the MPs.

Fyodor and I walked through the dark streets stumbling over rubble. I learned that he had been wounded twice, and that the Germans had killed his whole family. I told him about my family. We shared a history of loss. I felt great sympathy for him. It was hard for me to understand the hostility the Americans felt toward these men who had fought a common enemy with them and had suffered far greater losses.

The tables in the Femina were jammed with traders from the British, French, and Russian sectors. The noise blared through the padded door and the smoke of Camels, Philip Morrises, and Chesterfields clogged the air.

A German band accompanied a teenage singer in her rendition of *Lili Marlene.*

I saw Ridgeway, a first lieutenant with whom I had worked in Information and Records, sitting at a table littered with PX whiskey bottles, Coke bottles, empty glasses, and overflowing ashtrays.

I pulled Fyodor along as I pushed my way through the crowd to Ridgeway's table.

"Ridge, this is Fyodor. He wants to trade."

"Hey, Ruskie, sit down." Ridge made a sweeping motion with his hand. The music had stopped and two more Americans joined us with their German girlfriends.

We shared drinks and cigarettes and I explained what Fyodor wanted.

"I can't make him a clock out of those watches he has, but I can get a kitchen clock for them," Ridge said.

I explained to Fyodor what the offer was. With a grin exposing metal teeth, Fyodor offered half an arm of watches.

"Make it one full arm" countered Ridgeway.

"Okay," the Russian said.

We arranged to meet Ridge the next evening at the same place.

The following evening I met Fyodor at the door as arranged. Ridge was sitting in a far corner at a small table behind a Doric column. Fyodor followed me as I battled my way across the crowded dance floor. Ridge offered Fyodor and me a drink and cigarettes, which Fyodor gratefully accepted. A package, wrapped in *The Stars and Stripes*, was on the table. Ridge pushed it to Fyodor. He tore off the paper and exposed an old alarm clock that had two domes with small hammers under them attached to the top of its metal frame.

"What can it do?" Fyodor asked.

I translated to Ridge.

Ridge wound up the clock, set the alarm, placed the clock back on the table, and pressed the top button. The alarm jangled.

Fyodor watched the clock skip across the table as the four hammers vibrated against the two metal domes.

"Half an arm," he whispered to me in Russian.

"Half an arm," I said to Ridge.

"The deal's off. He promised one arm." Ridge took the clock off the table and began to wrap it up again.

"You promised a kitchen clock, which you indicated to be the size of soccer ball," I said. I still felt the sting of the humiliation Fyodor must have felt when Leahy laughed in his face.

Ridge was not amused. "Whose side are you on, anyway? I hear you're even feeding the Krauts in your house."

I was taken aback by his outburst and sought a righteous answer. Not finding one, I stuck to the clock issue.

"You did promise a kitchen clock."

"So, what if I did? He doesn't know the difference."

"I do."

"What's the matter with you? Are you a Ruskie and a Kraut lover?"

"They're human beings."

"Not by me, they ain't. I'd just as soon shoot the whole lot of them."

Ridge had been in many battles that had helped to destroy this country, with its hatred for Jews and gypsies, Communists and Catholics, Poles and Czechs—and here was hate reincarnated. I was stunned by Ridge's vehemence. I no longer wanted to deal with him, but felt committed to the promise I had made to Fyodor.

"Let me ask him something, before you start World War Three."

"Who's stopping you?"

I elicited from Fyodor that he wanted the clock. I suggested he offer one arm, and if that did not work, we would leave. He agreed.

"Fyodor is willing to give you one arm."

"Which arm?"

The watches were a mixture of expensive Swiss, German, and PX issue.

"Which arm, Fyodor?"

Fyodor rolled up the sleeve of his right arm and extended it across the table.

"Let's see the other arm."

Fyodor had both sleeves rolled up and his arms stretched across the table. Ridge turned one arm and then the other, studying the watches. The clock was sitting between Fyodor's arms when the front door exploded and four MPs burst through. The singer screamed and rushed behind the stage door. The orchestra stopped playing. Tables, bottles, and glasses rolled to the floor as soldiers from the four sectors of Berlin scrambled to the rear doors. Ridge knocked over the table as he jumped across chairs. He was lost in the crowd and shoved to the back door.

The clock rolled to the floor with one last peal of the alarm.

I pulled Fyodor behind the upturned table, where we shuddered, hidden by a column, and watched the MPs drive everyone through the back door into waiting vans. Then the place was empty. Spilled liquor and soda ran down the fallen tables and pooled on the floor strewn with cigarette butts and ashes.

Sweat was running down Fyodor's face. My armpits were wet and I had a hard time breathing.

The singer peeked through the stage door and looked around and then walked to center stage. Soon the orchestra filtered back on stage, but the Femina remained empty. The clock was lying on its side by the table leg. I picked it up and handed it to Fyodor. He grinned and stuck it in his tunic, it bulged as if he had swallowed a melon.

We crawled out from under the table and slowly worked our way to the stage, ready at any sign of danger to duck under anything that might shelter us from another raid. The singer was sympathetic to our plight and guided us to the back door. We exited into an alley. I gave her my cigarettes. She thanked me profusely.

The night was clear and cold as Fyodor and I walked under a canopy of stars towards the Russian sector. We parted at the "You Are Now Leaving the American Sector" sign. He stopped under a lamp and waved with one hand and held the bulge in his tunic with the other. His metallic grin flashed in the light. I stood at Checkpoint Charlie and waved back. He walked down the deserted street. I waited for him to disappear into the night.

The streets were dark and empty. The homeless had crawled into the hollowed ruins. Somewhere in the distance, drunken soldiers belted out a bawdy song. The otherwise eerie silence converged into an endless stretch of nothingness. I quickened my pace to get back to light and warmth. I was almost home when I heard a moan so weak that I thought my mind was deceiving me. I stopped and listened. A few paces ahead of me a bundle of something lay abandoned against my neighbor's garden gate. Apprehensively, I skirted around it trying to avoid it. Another moan. Fear of darkness and of death circulated through my skin and urged me to run, but something held me there. I turned back, bent down, and, as if someone might hear me in this desolate street, whispered, "Are you all right?"

A barely audible "yes," answered.

Reluctantly, I helped the bundle of rags to its feet. There was no resistance, only the weight of weakness. I put my arms around it and dragged it home. The tattered body of rags collapsed onto the floor. Exposed was an emaciated woman with short, matted, rust-colored hair. I ran into the kitchen, opened a can of Campbell's chicken noodle soup bought at the commissary merely for trading, and spooned it down her throat unheated and undiluted. She coughed and sputtered as she greedily gulped it down. Then she fell asleep where she sat.

I wondered whether she was one of those German women of the Lebensborn, the women who volunteered to be impregnated by the finest of the SS to bear children for the Reich? Or was she a victim of rape by the victorious troops? There were so many of those—children, grandmothers, mothers. Or was she an ordinary starving German? The question of why I was helping this German woman crossed my mind fleetingly.

When she awakened she sipped some milk and ate a piece of bread, chewing every bite innumerable times, savoring every morsel. I ran the bath and helped her get out of her rags. The bones protruded through a lax skin. Tattooed in blue inside her left arm was her prisoner's number. Her arms were so shriveled that the number was not legible. She noticed my discomfort and took the rags from my hand, dropped them on the floor.

"I was liberated from a camp near Prague," she said defiantly as she wobbled on her spindly legs to the bath.

"Theresienstadt," she added.

The word stunned me. This would be what my mother looked like. Something in my throat coagulated, bitter and caustic.

I washed her hair and scrubbed her the way Katja had scrubbed me in Gdynia, all the while choking on my fear. I wrapped a towel around her and led her to the living room. She sat on the floor hunched over, chewing on a buttered piece of bread. Her vacant blue eyes watched me warily. There was something hauntingly familiar about her. The washed hair had sprung into curls that capped her head. It recalled a person I had known long ago, but I could not grasp the place or time and strained to remember. My thoughts catapulted across the years to the last family dinner. Genia the dancer. Genia the woman of lithe body and white skin and hair that capped her head like woven copper. Could it be? The hair was rust-colored now, but the way it wove around her head was something known. The volcanic changes in my life had distorted the past, and I was no longer certain whether what I remembered was true or was a wild hallucination.

She took small bites from the bread slice, moving her hand sparingly to her mouth. Her eyes were empty of emotion. I was afraid to ask for fear of having hope denied, and yet I had to know.

"I knew someone a long time ago with hair like yours. Her name was Genia and she was my dancing teacher in Berlin and…" I would have gone on and on had not her gentle touch silenced me. Surprise brought life to her eyes and in a voice so soft I could hardly hear she asked:

"Are you Miriam?" The words were Czech now.

I did not remember that soft voice. I touched her wasted hand.

"Yes, I am."

She leaned forward and looked at me intently. "I don't recognize you."

"I was six then. I'm nineteen now."

There was no fluid left in her; her tears were soft moans. She gripped my hand tightly as if it were a life preserver. Trapped in the unearthly terrain of my mind were deformed memories.

"I thought you were lost. I thought everyone was lost." There was pain in her words and I absorbed the echo of that pain but sat motionless, transported to that time when the table gleamed with silver and glass and all I wanted was my cornucopia and Genia had admonished my father for his strictness. Words surrendered to the memory of those happy days and were no longer necessary. We sat for a long time.

Slowly, hesitantly she began to talk. She had been arrested in Paris and transported to Theresienstadt. She met Mother and Lex there, and for a while they tried to stay together.

"Do you remember what year you were taken to Theresienstadt?"

"1941 or '42 or even '43. I don't really remember. We lived from day to day, most often not knowing what year it was or how long we had been there."

She told her story slowly. In the last weeks of the war, there was panic in the camp as trains carried off more and more prisoners packed into cattle cars. Lex was on the first one to go.

"We did not know where they were going. Then they took Tilly. We did not know it then, but the war was coming to an end. If the train that took Tilly had been just four days later, she would have been liberated by the Russians as I was."

"Then Mutti might still be alive?"

"The trains never brought anyone back." There was a pause. Then she added, as if she had just remembered it, "The Russians freed me. I spent four years there. Don't know how I survived. I'm still not certain I'm here, and with you."

I had just lost my consoling thought that Mother had not died in an extermination camp but perhaps had a "normal" death in the "model prison" of Theresienstadt

A vast sadness spread into the empty spaces of my body like a crimson stain. I could not move or say anything. Before me lay the unacceptable story of Mutti's and Lex's deaths.

I moved toward her and held her in my arms, this bundle of bones. Tears were trapped in my throat. I could not let them go in front of her. They seemed such an affront to human suffering. I rose and brought her more milk. She held the cup in both her hands and sipped slowly.

After liberation, she had walked from Prague to Berlin, sometimes catching a ride in someone's wagon, twice on the handlebars of a bicycle, and always going wherever they were going, often having to backtrack. She wanted to get to Leipzig. She was looking for her husband and daughter there, where she had last seen them. The hope of a reunion with them flickered in her wasted body and urged her onward. The odds of her making it to Leipzig or finding her family were against her. I pleaded with her to stay, at least till she was well.

"I will stay two days."

Surprised at the firmness of her voice, I realized that nothing could keep her from her quest.

Light trickled through the window dispelling some of the terrors of the night in spite of the ruins so clearly silhouetted against the sky.

I fed her every two hours, bread and milk and soup. She recovered a little, but I did not believe her to be strong enough to go anywhere, yet I could not convince her to stay.

I bought some clothes and a ticket to Leipzig. Two days later she was dressed and ready to go. I stuffed a duffel bag full of bread, canned goods, and cartons of cigarettes. The cigarettes would buy her sustenance for a long time.

We walked to the station arm in arm, mine supporting her weak body.

I sat on a bench on the platform and watched Genia's emaciated arm wave until the train vanished. There was a blockage in my veins choking off my blood. I wondered where Genia was going to end. For that matter, where was I going to end? I knew that wherever that would be, it would never be permanent, because it would be snatched from me by some sudden turn of events created by men I did not know.

Eventually, the signs of East-West hostilities began and the sectors were closed off from one another.

Tiny and Spike were going home. I accompanied them to the train that would take them to Bremerhaven. His duffel bag thrown over his shoulder, Spike hugged me. Tiny suddenly swooped me up in his arms and swung me around and around. We laughed and cried.

Eyes brimming with tears, Tiny said: "Sure glad I'm leaving this hellhole."

"If you do decide to come to the States, you look me up, hear? And don't become a ward of the state," Spike said, grinning.

The train pulled in. Spike and Tiny threw their duffel bags into the corridor and leaned out of the window. As the train pulled out, both were swinging their caps out of the window, shouting, "Good luck."

I waved till the train vanished around a curve, and wondered whether I would ever decide to go to the States.

Within a year the occupation troops and their dependents had replaced the warriors. Following the time-honored precepts of the pukka sahib, they scrupulously avoided unnecessary contact with the Germans except for the Frauleins and the swarms of hungry Germans who attended upon them as maids, waiters, janitors, and the like. All posters warning of venereal disease were dutifully removed, some clubs were closed, scrip money was issued, and the wives formed their usual clubs. Berlin lost its glitter.

I had received a letter from Nora in Czechoslovakia telling me that she had information about Mother. I had replied and asked her to explain, but she wrote that it was not something she could tell me in a letter. There were no phone lines to Prague and I decided that I had to go there to find out.

Colonel Leahy sat behind his desk lighting a fresh cigar with the butt of another. He blew the smoke toward ceiling. "You want to go where?"

"Prague, sir, to see my sister."

"That's occupied by the Russians," he said.

"I'll take the chance."

He crushed the butt in his overflowing ashtray, leaned across his desk, and frowned at me. "We could have had that whole damn country, if Washington hadn't ordered us to halt at Pilzen. There we sat, waiting for the Ruskies to capture Prague."

"I had nothing to do with it, sir."

"Goddamn right." He sat down again.

"May I have a TDY, sir?"

The exiled Czech government in London had issued me a passport. That little booklet had turned me from a stateless nonentity into a bona fide living human person. In order to let him know that I was validated with a piece of paper, I said, "I can use my Czech passport once I'm there."

"For Chrissake, you use your passport and they won't let you out of the damn country."

"Okay, I won't use my passport, sir."

He cranked the telephone and bellowed. "Issue a TDY for Darvas—two weeks!"

"Thank you, sir."

He leaned back in his chair, folded his hands across his belly, and grinned. "Train only goes to the German border."

"Then I'll be back in a couple of days."

His grin became wider. "You'll be back sooner."

The more direct route to Prague was a two-hundred-mile run through Dresden. Since Dresden had been totally destroyed, no traffic throughout that city was possible. The alternate route was a five-hundred-mile detour south to Nürnberg, then backtracking north to the border.

The train was packed with shabbily clad people, their faces tormented by hunger and fear. I guarded my two duffel bags stuffed with cartons of cigarettes by sitting on them in the corridor. The train moved sluggishly through devastated country, stopping at every village. The only food and water available was hawked at the stops for cigarettes. Hundreds of hands reached for the open windows displaying their wares: shriveled potatoes, wilted carrots, water ladled from tin buckets. I bought a bucket of water and a loaf of bread for a carton of cigarettes. I wanted to share the bread, but it was ripped out of my hands before I could distribute it.

Alighting in Nürnberg three days later, I was faint from thirst. People piled off the train, stampeding to sell their cherished possessions for a gulp of water. Five cigarettes bought me an apple, a ladle of water, and a raw potato.

As in Berlin, the rubble had been cleared from the streets.

The only solid building was the restored courthouse where the trials were in progress. Guarded by MPs in white, spotless webbed belts and leggings, the building oozed justice. An oppressive sense of expectation hung over the city.

The mess hall was like a four-star restaurant. I ate till I was ready to burst, bought some K-rations, and stayed at a military hotel long enough for a bath. Returning to the station, I sat on a wooden bench, guarding my duffel bags, and waiting for the connection to Prague. An MP sat down beside me. We chatted about this and that. He was returning to Berlin. I told him I was going to Prague.

"What! You're going where?"

"Prague."

I watched a familiar wooden caboose ease into the station. The conductor's whistle hung from his lapel as he leaned out of the caboose. I picked up my duffel bags.

The MP grabbed my arm. "Don't you know that's Russian territory?"

"We're allies," I said and removed his hand.

"You kidding?"

"We've got troops in Pilzen."

"Yeah, but the Czechs are pissed at us."

"What about?"

"We handed General Vlasov over to the Russians. They executed him."

"What can they do to me?"

"If the Czechs don't think of something, the Russians will. They don't want us here."

"Here's my train."

"I wouldn't go there in that uniform."

"Thanks for the information."

"You're nuts," the MP called as I boarded.

As we backtracked north, the landscape that glided past the dirty window disturbed me. Though I did not remember where my family and I had crossed the border, the scene was oppressive.

"Where are you going?" the conductor asked.

"Prague," I replied, not certain I wanted to continue the journey.

"This train does not cross the border."

I nodded.

"No one travels this route. Don't know why we run it. The border tracks are full of Germans."

"What are they doing there?"

"They've been expelled from Czechoslovakia."

"Poetic justice," I said.

"An eye for an eye. They live in the cattle cars they used to use to transport Jews to concentration camps."

He sat down beside me. I offered him a cigarette, and we smoked and watched the landscape. It was not familiar, but then I had been on foot when I last crossed that border. Memories of that time tumbled through my head and, for a moment, my breath was trapped in my chest. I wanted to get off the train.

The engine chugged to a stop. "This is it," the conductor said.

"There's no station," I said.

"Station's across the border in Cheb, about ten miles."

No sooner had I stepped onto the tracks than the train backed out and disappeared around a curve, its chimney belching smoke.

To the right and left cattle cars covered the landscape. Cauldrons steamed over open flames, filling the air with a noxious odor.

People dressed in rags, begging for food, surrounded me. I was overwhelmed by their poverty and passed out my Krations. Then I wondered what had compelled me to aid these people who had marched to Hitler's drummers.

A group of displaced Germans followed me to the border. One man kept pace by my side.

"I'm just a butcher. I knew nothing of what was going on," he said, tears streaming down his face.

That was the theme of every German I had met. Not one admitted to knowing anything about what had happened, nor did the men admit to fighting at the Western Front. The whole Wehrmacht, according to their stories, had been fighting the Russians on the Eastern Front. I regretted handing out my K-rations.

The butcher and the rest of them stopped at the border and watched me walk through the Bohemian Forest. I met no one on the long trek until I came to an unfamiliar village. Just beyond the village, on a siding, sat a wooden railway car with smoke drifting from a chimney. Raucous singing and laughter blasted through the open windows and doors.

I climbed in. The train was full of Czech soldiers sitting around a potbellied stove, passing wine bottles and slicing salami with bayonets.

"Hey, look, an American has fallen from heaven!" the one with the bayonet said.

The singing stopped. All turned to stare. One soldier moved the bottle from his mouth and with wine dripping down his chin said, "Goddam, a girl." His eyes were round as marbles.

"Bet you she has cigarettes," another said, and put two fingers to his mouth and inhaled air as a signal to the American.

"Hi, fellas," I said in Czech.

Stunned silence.

Suddenly, I was surrounded. Questions about my uniform, cigarettes, what I was doing there flew at me. One pushed the men away from me and offered me a seat. Someone thrust a bottle at me.

"Go on, take a swig," said the one with the salami.

I took a swig. He handed me a slice of salami on his bayonet.

We sat around the stove. Several bottles of wine and and a few salamis made the rounds while we sang Czech folk songs so loudly the sound must have traveled across the border. Smoke filled the wagon from the packages of cigarettes I passed around.

Petr, the one who had offered me the first bite of salami, asked me what I was doing in Selb. At least now I knew where I was.

"I need to get to Prague."

"You have to get to Cheb. Good five-mile walk."

"Which way is it?"

"We'll get you there," said Jiri, the one who passed the bottle.

"There's a train from Cheb to Pilzen," Vladimir said.

"I want to go to Prague."

"You change trains in Pilzen," Petr said.

Escorted by twenty-four Czech soldiers carrying my depleted duffel bags. I walked the five miles to Cheb through woods and across fields, through tiny hamlets and across railroad tracks. When we arrived in Cheb, we danced and sang up and down the platform until the train arrived. The villagers gathered on the tracks. Some clapped, some sang along, others shook their heads.

The soldiers loaded me on the decrepit train and crowded into the compartment. My hand hurt from all the handshakes. When the whistle blew, one after an other jumped off the train. I leaned out of the window and waved. The soldiers waved and whistled. Then they disappeared behind a copse of trees.

I alighted in Pilzen. The train to Prague was not due in for six hours. I left the station in search of a restaurant. The town felt tense. The streets were devoid of traffic. Pedestrians hurried to their destinations hunched into their overcoats. I stopped a man. "Can you recommend a restaurant?"

He looked behind him. "They're closed," he said, and rushed away.

I walked back to the station and sat on the bench with a growling stomach.

Two Czech policemen entered the station and walked toward me. Here was help. I rose, walked toward them smiling. "Papers," said one grim policeman.

I showed him my TDY orders. The document had an official stamp on it, and any bureaucrat worth his salt knew an official stamp signified authority.

He looked over my TDY order. He shook his head and handed it to the other one. They looked at me and shook their heads. A moment later I was in a police car.

"I'm going to Prague on an interpreting job."

No response.

"I'm going to miss the train," I said.

Silence.

I was locked into a cell. The bulb dangling from the ceiling, the window high above, the toilet in the corner, weakened my legs. My intestines turned somersaults.

Two Americans were sitting on a cot and looked up with interest.

"Hi, what brought you here?" one asked. His name was Gerald. The other was Jim.

"I don't know." I was going to be sick.

"They say some Americans robbed the castle."

I vomited into the toilet. Gerald helped me sit down on the chained plank.

When I had sufficiently recovered, I asked what the Americans were supposed to have stolen.

"Jewelry," Gerald replied.

"Did they?"

"No. This is reprisal for our handing their general over to the Russians."

"Why you?"

"We were outside the American compound."

"What next?"

"Guess our commanding officer will get us out."

The door opened. Immediately my body stiffened. A policeman set down a tray with a large bowl of thick soup, three slices of bread, and three cups of coffee, and left. I relaxed. We ate the soup. The bread reminded me of the bread Angelika and I had eaten at the peasant woman's house.

Gerald said that the colonel could not get me out of jail as I was not assigned to their outfit. Since there was no chance that Gerald and Jim's commanding officer could or would rescue me, I had to do it myself and soon.

I asked the policeman to permit me to talk to the chief. The policeman nodded and returned to lead me to him.

The chief rose and shook hands. "I understand you speak Czech."

"Yes, sir." He was impressed with the "sir." I silently thanked Colonel Leahy for his lesson.

"You are not from this base?"

"I'm from Berlin and need to get to Prague for an interpreting job."

That's what Leahy had told me to say were I to make it to Prague.

Again I presented the document issued by Colonel Leahy. He took it, studied it carefully and handed it back. "These papers are not acceptable."

I had been traveling for five days. Getting to Prague would take one or two more days, the return trip another six or seven. I would be AWOL again. I had no idea how long I might sit in that cell. Considering my options I had no other choice.

I passed my passport across the desk.

He looked up surprised. "So, you're Czech."

"Yes, sir."

"And you're working for the Americans in Berlin?"

"Yes, sir."

He leafed through the passport. I lit a cigarette and blew the smoke toward him. He watched with an addict's longing.

He threw the passport on his desk and leaned forward. "This passport was issued by the Czech provisional government in London."

That was the fly in the soup. Hoping to soften his disapproval, I offered him a cigarette. He stared at the package of Camels and shook his head.

I laid it in front of him. "Take the pack."

He picked up the package and turned it in his hand, pronouncing the word "camel" as "tsamel." I took out my Zippo lighter and flicked it. He removed a cigarette from the pack as if he were handling a precious and fragile object, rolled it under his nose and closed his eyes, then leaned forward for the light. Leaning his head against the backrest, he inhaled and blew the smoke out with a sigh.

He watched the smoke drift to the ceiling, then looked at me, his eyes cold. "Those cowards escaped to save their own hide."

"Which cowards?"

"The bureaucrats. The government. The people who could afford to get out."

The resentment in his voice shook me. "I was too young to be a coward."

"Your parents weren't."

"My parents died in a concentration camp."

His eyes softened. "Good American cigarettes," he said and lit another one. While he smoked, he seemed to be considering something.

I cursed myself for having used my passport, and wished I had listened to Leahy.

He studied the cigarette as he rolled it between his thumb and index finger with satisfaction.

Without looking up or ceasing to roll the cigarette, he said suddenly, "I'll let you go to Prague."

I folded my arms across my chest and waited for the catch.

"You'll need an exit visa."

"I assume I can get that in Prague?"

"Unfortunately, we do not issue exit visas to Czech citizens." He grinned.

So that was the catch. A captured citizen.

I put another pack of cigarettes on the desk. He took it without hesitation. I took a deep breath.

"Can you issue a visa?"

"No, but I will drive you to the station."

At least the cigarettes paid for a ride.

At the Pilzen station I learned that I had missed the daily train by two hours. For twenty-two hours I either slept on the bench or walked up and down the platform. I bought two stale rolls and a cup of water from a vendor for a pack of cigarettes. He charged me an extra pack to keep the cup.

At last the train pulled in. I lounged in the comparative comfort of the shabby compartment, too excited to sleep. Rain ran in dirty rivulets down the windows. Going home. The words beat in my head with the metallic click of the wheels. I leaned back and rested my shoulder against the wall. A silver curtain obscured the landscape. The window was streaked with the gray of muddy rain. The view faded into cracked images. How had it been? I had been so certain that it had been indelibly engraved in my mind, but nothing seemed to fit. What exactly did I think I was going to find in Prague? Did I expect to find people in mourning, wearing black to commemorate the day I had last seen my mother?

The sense of oppression persisted. Scenes of the border crossing, of Mother and Father flashed through my head like a remembered nightmare. Again I saw images of Steffie reaching out of the truck. Sadness descended on me like a veil. The monotonous clack-clack of the train hammered home that I was alone. Loneliness lay upon me like death.

November 1945

Return to Prague

At last, the city of a thousand spires sped toward me. Smudged Hradcany Castle passed by. The spires of the churches reached toward the sky. The city sparkled in gothic splendor, hiding the terror of yesterday in its narrow streets.

At the Wilson station I took a taxi to the Alcron Hotel. I had to bribe the clerk with a pack of cigarettes for a room. I chose the Alcron because it had been a hangout for journalists and writers and I had often gone there with Father to meet his colleagues. The marble staircase leading up to the rooms was still impressive. The red carpet patterned with gold and green fronds looked a bit worn, but the ghosts of my father's friends drifted by as I walked up the stairs to my room.

I lounged in the tub soaking off the seven-day dirt and grime and hoped the images of the past would vanish, but they persisted. I called Lilka.

We were both so excited that neither of us could stop talking. Vaclav would be home tomorrow night and I was to come for dinner. They had something to tell me.

I crawled into bed and slept. Awakened from a fitful sleep, momentarily unaware of my surroundings, I dressed and went to the hotel restaurant.

The dining room was full. The waiter asked if I objected to sharing a table with a gentleman.

"Certainly not," I said. He led me to the very table where I had sat with my father and Uncle Egon and Lex. I felt insubstantial and could not move. The waiter pulled out the chair for me and the man at the table rose.

"Good morning," he said. He was a British correspondent on assignment in Prague. His name was Brian Storm. I told him that I had sat at this very table with my father. While he buttered his roll, he said in a low voice, "Better change into civvies."

"I don't have any."

"Get some."

We exchanged a few stories and parted.

I walked across the Charles Bridge. I used to skip across it as a child, bowing to the statues flanking its parapets. The river swirled beneath the bridge, flotsam bobbing on it. Women, their heads covered with babushkas, walked past me carrying their net bags filled with groceries they had bartered for at the market. They turned to look at me. Russian soldiers, walking in pairs, stared at the "American." I decided to take the Briton's advice. I crossed the market that had once been filled with farmers in colorful costumes to the Old Town Square and walked across the Staromestke namesti past the monument to Jan Hus. In a small shop in Paris Street I bought a dress and a coat, and wore it out of the store. It did not fit well, as the Czechs are short and round. The shoulders drooped and the waist was too large, but I felt safer. I carried my uniform wrapped in newspaper.

Passing the Tyn cathedral that commands the Old Town Square, I remembered passing it on my way to school, and how Angelika and I used to bend back trying to see the spires jutting into the sky. Angelika, my dear friend, dead among the ashes of war and hatred. I stopped at the old clock, the Orloj, and watched and watched the small windows on top, waiting for the figures to appear. Pale rays of sun forced their way through a gray sky and shimmered on the closed windows of the Orloj. I shivered and turned away from the clock to walk the narrow streets.

I wandered up Vaclavske namesti and stopped before St. Wenceslaus sitting on his horse guarding the chestnut-lined namesti before him. The National Museum rose behind him. I thought of Minna and wondered what had befallen her. I could not remember where her apartment had been, but I did remember the Nazi flag that had been placed in St. Wenceslaus's hand.

Behind the National Museum lay a section of the city where street names had an international flavor: Italian Street, Yugoslav Street, English Street. It was at Spanish Street 6 that I had last seen Mother at home. Urged on by conflicting emotions, I walked to the left of the museum down Vynohradska Street and turned right into Spanelska. The building where I had once lived looked dreary and cold.

I remembered that, as a child, I would crouch with a pitcher of water over the rainspout on the balcony of the third floor and wait for an opportune moment to drench a passerby. One particular day, when I had been crouching in wait for a victim, a woman passed beneath the balcony. I poured the pitcher through the spout. The water splattered on the woman's shoulder. She stopped, looked up, shook her fist at the balcony, and cursed. I quickly disappeared behind the balcony door and hid behind the curtains, leaving the pitcher on the balcony. On the street was a telltale puddle trickling into the gutter.

I smiled at the memory and kept looking at the balcony. The iron balconies jutting over the street were rusted. Only their ornate design proclaimed their once fashionable status.

I walked into an empty entrance hall. Once there had been a table in the center of the hall supporting a vase of flowers. The old tile floor echoed under my steps, making a hollow sounds. The tall windows in the center of the landings had become opaque with years of dirt, and they cast a shadowed light. On the third floor I rang the bell to the apartment that had been my home. A woman opened the door a mere crack.

"What do you want?" the hoarse voice said.

"I used to live here," I said.

"So?"

"May I come in for a moment?"

Reluctantly she opened the door and stepped aside. I looked at the place where my father's bookshelves had been, the windowsill where the vase of flowers used to stand. I walked to the balcony and looked across the street into the park where I had played as a child. I turned back to the apartment. Everything was unraveling and I knew I was back there in the tomblike silence of aloneness.

The woman had followed me and watched me suspiciously. I looked around me. The years had cleaned away all traces of my parents' life.

"All the people who lived here then are dead now," I said. The woman nodded her head but said nothing.

I excused myself and walked out the door and down the stairs. Faster and faster I walked until I was running. I felt I was going to suffocate unless I got away.

I ran to the Riegrove Sady, my lungs bursting. The park was deserted. I walked along the path winding up the hill and sat on a bench by a sandbox where Nora and I had often played. My thoughts were incoherent. One picture after another flashed through my mind as I viewed the surroundings in which I had lived. Through the drizzle the castle on the hill across town seemed to dissolve.

I sat there for a long time. Rain dripped down my face and neck and ran into my coat collar. Anxiety permeated my whole body. Quickly, I walked back to Vaclavske namesti. I wished I hadn't come.

I stopped at the Julius Meindl coffeehouse on Vaclavske namesti where Mother used to buy her coffee. Perhaps the original Meindl was gone, too. I ordered a cup of coffee and waited for the grounds to settle in the strong mahogany brew. My hands shook as I lifted the cup. The crowd flowed by languidly, apathetically, like a sluggish river. In front of the Hotel Europa a woman was selling lilies-of-the-valley. I felt incorporeal, hovering between the past and present.

"Konvalinky," the woman sang to the passersby, "Buy some konvalinky."

Mother used to have lilies-of-the-valley sitting in small vases in her bedroom.

I leaned against a chestnut tree. The street looked smudged and dreamlike through my tears as I walked slowly along the wet pavement to the hotel. I was only dimly aware of the shapes of buildings that leaned in on me from both sides of the street, threatening to crush me.

I stepped into the shower and hoped the water beating down on me would wash away the pain of memory. The spray stung my cold body like a thousand needles.

My dress and coat were wet, but rather than wear my uniform, I put them on again and walked to Lilka's.

The door opened instantly as if Lilka had been standing behind it waiting. We fell into each other's arms.

"You haven't changed at all," Lilka said, holding me at arm's length.

"You haven't changed either, considering it's only been two years."

"Come in. Vaclav is anxious to see you."

She closed the door. The apartment was bare except for a table and four chairs.

Vaclav and I greeted each other with a kiss and a hug.

I looked around. "Are you moving?"

Two candles dripped from empty wine bottles, and the light from the street lamp flickered through the lace curtains, giving the room a haunted feeling.

"I'll tell you about it, but let's have wine first."

We sat around the table, drank wine, and ate cheese. Lilka and I talked and laughed and cried. We reminisced about our years in England; wondered where the Rosenblums's daughters were; and laughed about the burial of the dishes and mused about the different turns our lives had taken. We avoided any reference to our mothers. Vaclav swirled the wine and studied his glass. He remained silent. The flower-shaped pattern of the lace curtains was etched against the dark windowpane. The air was tense, laden with secrets. I drank more wine and watched the light on the windowsill.

"They're canceling the pilot licenses of ex-RAF flyers," Vaclav said, still watching the swirls in his wineglass.

"What do you mean?"

"They're accusing the flyers who fought in England of having fought for capitalism, and they're sending them to the mines in Slovakia. Re-education, they call it. Can you believe it?" Lilka answered.

Vaclav stared into his glass.

"Father left yesterday," Lilka said.

"How did he get out?"

"He's walking to Germany."

"I don't think he'll have a problem," I said. "The border is unguarded, at least where I crossed. But I have a problem. I came in on my passport and am supposed to get an exit visa."

Vaclav looked up from his glass. "You can't get an exit visa," he said.

"I know. The policeman in Pilzen pointed that out to me."

The silence was charged with tension. The wind beat against the window and the streetlamp glittered like a distant star.

"We're leaving," Vaclav said. The sound of his voice cracked the silence like splintering glass. "It won't be long before I will lose my pilot's license and be sent to the mines."

"Where are you going?"

Vaclav poured more wine. "We made a mistake returning."

"We're going back to England," Lilka said.

"If you can't get an exit visa and there are no flights out of here, how—"

Vaclav did not wait for me to finish the sentence. "I'm to fly to Brno Friday morning and pick up the minister of trade and bring him back."

"Instead you're flying to London?"

"Right."

"Do you have room for me?"

"It's risky. Do you want to take the chance?" Vaclav asked.

I did not have to think about my reply. "I'm coming. I still have time to visit Nora." I had still not had time to get the news that could not be put into a letter.

"She lives in Holice, about a five-hour train ride from here," Lilka said.

"I can take the train and be back by Thursday."

"You'll be pushing it," Vaclav said.

"Maybe I should take the chance on getting out later."

"You won't have a chance later," Vaclav said. "They're closing the borders."

"You better come with us," said Lilka.

"I'll be back, if I have to hitchhike."

"If you don't make it, we'll have to leave without you," Vaclav said.

"I'll make it."

The train was like all the old trains I had traveled on. Though the countryside was beautiful, it was all very depressing.

At Holice, Nora stood on the platform with her baby buggy. Her six-month-old daughter Jana slept peacefully in the comfort of her warm blanket. I wondered what her future would be. The world, wrote Voltaire, is a vast shipwreck, and I hoped that my generation might be able to repair it for her.

Nora led me through the unpaved village streets to the small hut where she lived with her in-laws. We exchanged greetings and had coffee. Then Nora and I walked through the village, leaving the baby in the care of her grandparents.

I realized she was unhappy. "You should have come to Berlin with me," I said.

"I was in love," Nora said. "Don't you remember?"

I remembered. I did not remind her that I had thought then that she should not return to Prague.

"You're not in love anymore?"

"Vaclav is working in the mines in Slovakia to be re-educated to Communism and I have not seen him for a year. We're getting divorced."

"What are you going to do?"

"I don't know."

We sat on a bench by the village pond and watched ducks waddle across the road to the pond. The frogs croaked in the pond and somewhere a dog barked. The sun was gone. A breeze filtered through the trees.

"I have the affidavit of Mother's death," Nora finally said.

"I thought she died in Theresienstadt."

"She did not die there. By the way, the name Theresienstadt has been changed back to the Czech name of Terezin."

"Where then?"

Nora shivered and rose. We walked back to the house.

"Where did she die?"

Nora brought a piece of flimsy paper out of a drawer and solemnly handed it to me. "That's the affidavit you think might bring you consolation. I had to go to the Central Archives in Prague to get it."

I opened the piece of yellowing paper. The print was faded and the cheap paper was crumbling at the folds.

Nora continued her story as I carefully smoothed the paper.

"This arrogant official said to me, 'You want to know where your mother died? That's years ago. A lot has changed. The files are not organized.' I handed him the five dollars you sent me. 'I have to rummage in the basement, come back in two days,' he said to me."

I held the paper and stared at the heading:

"STATE CENTRAL ARCHIVES OF PRAGUE"

I heard Nora's voice as if I were underwater.

"Two days later I am again facing this dour official in his tattered uniform. He tells me that he has had no time. I give him another five dollars. Miraculously, the document appears from his desk drawer. It's in Czech. Can you still read it?"

"Of course." I began to translate:

"Notice, that piece of official paper made her of Jewish nationality and spelled her name the Polish way," Nora said. But I heard her only dimly. I began to translate.

STATE CENTRAL ARCHIVES OF PRAGUE

Subject: Matylda Darvasova—certificate of deportation. The State Central Archive herewith informs you, that according to the information in the files, persons of Jewish nationality were deported during the occupation. Matylda Darvasova, born 14.12.1900, last address Praha II Poric c. 10, was deported on 30.11.1941 with transport number H 717 to Theresienstadt. On 9.1.1942 she was further transported by transport number O 712 to Riga. No further information on prisoners is to be found in this archive. We caution that evidence of prisoners is not complete, because German officials destroyed most of the files in 1945.

My mind recoiled from the immediate vision brought on by the word Riga.

Riga, an obscure town sitting in a sandy hollow near the Baltic, is the capital of Latvia. Fought over for whatever reason men believed important, it was controlled at various times by Poles, Swedes, Russians, and Germans. The Germans had made it famous as a synonym for death. It had become a monument to efficient, state-sanctioned murder.

A heavy familiar sadness washed over me, making me ill. Ache and anger tightened in a band around my chest and constricted my breath. I wanted my mother and father back. I wanted it all to have been a nightmare, I wanted to weep but only a dry rattle escaped my lungs. I had no tears left. I would gladly have died for them.

My sweet, gentle, fastidious mother had died an ignominious death in filth and despair. The thought drove me out of the house. I rushed out into the village street and walked and walked till I came to the woods. I sat down on a hillock and tried to shake the image of Mutti sitting motionless among the skeletons, the skin over her shaven skull covering an emaciated head, bones like dead and broken sticks, her blank eyes watching with terror the trucks that gather human beings to be fed into their ovens and their gas chambers. And Father. What happened to him? Nothing about him. Not his name. Not where he went, not where he died. The solid, firm man of my childhood was gone as if he had never lived. A wayfarer leaving no footprints.

As I sat on the hillock, a pounding, simmering fury bubbled through my veins threatening to drive me insane. I pressed my fists against my temples, trying to tranquilize my raw nerves. Poisoning rage begun years before was released in a violent flow of tears. They poured through my locked fingers. The raw, numbing anguish of two generations of loss and disappointment coagulated in my veins. A part of me died eternally on that hillock.

I needed to control these raw feelings. If I did not, the world would unhinge. I made my way back through the woods, stumbled into the village square, and sat down on the bench by the pond. Ducks swam in secure calm, creating little concentric circles. I sat for a long time till the quiet of the pond, the woods, and the ducks slowed my drumming blood. Nothing ever happened here, I thought, and I resented not having been able to live out my life as it might have been.

When I was able to control my thoughts, I walked back to Nora's. Her eyes were red. Her shoulders jerked convulsively. I could hardly watch her pain. I embraced her. What consolation was there?

"It happened to millions," I said.

"She was not millions," Nora said and disengaged herself from my arms. "That's supposed to be a consolation?" Her eyes were angry.

"I am sorry," I said. Tears ran down my face. Nora sat with her hands in her lap and looked at me through her red-rimmed eyes.

"I could not have made the choice of sending my daughter away without knowing what might happen to her," Nora said.

I realized then the anguish that choice had cost my mother. The pain ripped through my very bones. I was overcome by Nora's weeping. That ratty piece of paper had confirmed Mother's death with an official seal of certainty and opened the door to suppressed pain.

"Was there a dream in all those nightmares?" I whispered into the darkening room.

"I don't remember any."

We had tapped into our wounds and tried to ward off the pain with silence.

Once more I slept under a kitchen table haunted by images of Mother and Father. Next morning Nora and I walked to the station.

"I'll see you soon," Nora said, embracing me.

I knew we would not see one another again for a long time, perhaps never.

"Soon," I said and boarded the train.

The clack of the train's wheels shouted of death and despair. Black boots marched through my head, and arms whipped my mother in unrelenting cadence. My mind shouted stop, stop. I wanted to pull the emergency brake and get off the train to flee. Where to? Flee from myself, from the images? There was no escape from the poisonous rage and pain.

I walked in the rain from the station to the Alcron Hotel. The cold, stabbing rain mingled with my angry tears and calmed me.

I took a shower, left my uniform hanging over a chair, grabbed my bag, checked out, and took a taxi to Lilka's.

"How was your visit?" Lilka asked.

"Fine." I could not bring myself to talk about it.

We spent the night talking with a nervous and irrational excitement about everything but our fears. Vaclav fidgeted and brooded. His hands moved nervously when he instructed us in what to do.

"You and Lilka get into the hangar and hide there while I distract the mechanic. The plane will be on the tarmac. I will walk there as usual. When the propeller roars full blast, you run like hell."

We sat at the table in mourning. Everything they had hoped for, everything they had dreamed of, was destroyed once again.

Dawn was a gray streak across the horizon. Vaclav drove us through empty streets. The drumming of rain on the roof of the car and the purring of the engine was the only sound on silent roads. Rain sleeted against the headlights. I kept looking behind, certain that we were being followed, but saw only the black curtain of the night.

Vaclav let us off a few yards from the entrance to the airfield. We hid behind the shrubbery lining the back of the hangar. Rain splashed on the black leaves, stirring up a lingering sense of danger. When the car's taillights were extinguished and we saw Vaclav talking to the mechanic, we ran in a low crouch, hugging the shadows of the shrubbery, and hid in the hangar.

The rain drummed down on the tin roof and washed Vaclav's image into a silvery tint that seemed to hang in the air like a ghost. The single-engine, two-seater plane was a smudged shadow on the tarmac. The asphalt looked like a black lake and Vaclav seemed to be swimming across it, his figure flickering like an old movie reel. Every shadow, every sound made me shiver. Lilka was gripping my arm. Vaclav's shadowy figure rushed into the cockpit. The propeller's stutter shattered the silence. I looked at Lilka. Her eyes were the size of wagon wheels staring at the plane.

"Come on, come on," Lilka pleaded with the propellers.

My heart bounced inside my chest, ready to explode. I knew all of Prague could hear that engine building to a roar and that soon we would be discovered.

At last the blades twirled at full speed. Lilka, longer of limb than I was, sprinted across the tarmac. She pulled herself into the seat behind Vaclav. Out of breath, I climbed onto Lilka's lap and closed the hatch.

The mechanic came running out of the office. I could see him in the shaft of light breaking through the door. His arms waving, he shouted something. His words were lost in the sound of the engine.

The plane rolled across the field, then rose slowly into the rain. We flew high across the mountains. The turbulence bounced the plane up and down and Lilka and I clutched each other. "I hope we make it," she shouted in my ear. "I hope so, too," I shouted back. The blood rushed into my head with the excitement of fear. Then the plane stopped quaking. We sailed smoothly across Germany and we relaxed. The country flowed beneath me like a swiftly flowing river. Prague was behind me. I felt a jab of pain knowing suddenly that I would never be able to return. The feeling persisted even after we landed at London's Croydon airport in a drizzling fog.

It took several days for the officials to verify our story and a few more for me to get a new uniform. We stayed at a pension, compliments of the British government, which was grateful for the return of their expensively-trained Czech flyer.

I flew back to Berlin as soon as a military flight was available and immediately reported to Leahy.

He was puffing on a cigar when I reported for duty.

"You're AWOL again."

"I know, sir."

He leaned forward. "Don't tell me you landed in Paris again."

"No, sir. London."

He leaned back in his chair and rolled his eyes. "How the hell did you get to London?"

"Plane, sir."

He squinted and pointed his stubby finger at me. "There are no planes from Prague."

"There was one, sir."

"For an ACE. Ha!"

"A secret one, sir."

"Some kind of mess you got yourself into?"

"I had to use my passport, sir."

"Darvas, you're worse than an adventurer. You're a female adventurer."

"Is that bad, sir?"

"In my book it is."

"There are other books, sir."

He rolled his cigar to the corner of his mouth and pointed his finger at me like a pistol. "You're a smart-ass."

"Sorry, sir."

"Women have no business in uniform."

He rose and walked to the window. His hands folded behind him, he stared out for some time. I wondered what was coming.

He moved to the front of the desk, leaned against it, and studied me. I stepped back and wished there were something I could lean against.

He folded his arms across his chest and sat on the edge of his desk, one foot on the floor, the other swinging with annoyance. "My tour is up next month, thank God!"

What was I supposed to say? "That's nice, sir," or "Too bad, sir," or "Good luck, sir"? I shifted from one foot to the other, wondering where this was going.

"Sit down." He walked around his desk.

I sat on the edge of the chair, anticipating another outburst.

He pushed his cigarette box toward me. "Have one."

I took one and lit it. I kept my feet firmly planted on the floor.

"Darvas, you've been a pain in the butt."

"Life is unpredictable, sir."

"Well, yours may be."

I saw his life as being one easy flow from childhood to manhood to warrior. No accidents or deviations allowed.

"I'm going to overlook this escapade of yours."

He looked to the window. Then, as if he had remembered something, he turned to face me. "Oh, and Darvas, if you ever get to the States, please don't look me up."

His laughter followed me through the door.

The day he left, he threw me a salute. The last of the warriors was gone.

184

Six months later my contract expired and I left Berlin on a crisp May day and landed in London in a soupy fog.

London had a tattered appearance but was definitely an improvement over Berlin. The Czech government and the Czech Red Cross had been repatriated. I found a place in Kensington Gardens Square, not much better than the rooms Lilka and I had shared during the tumultuous days of war.

Out of habit, I stored my suitcase under the bed. It was hardly worth unpacking the few belongings I had acquired over the years. Then I went out in search of the Polish restaurant. It was still there in the alley, but now had a larger menu. The proprietor was happy to see me and asked about Lilka. I told him she and her husband were in London, but would soon be posted with the Royal Air Force to Riyadh.

"Then all's well," he said.

For days I pondered the possibilities. I could stay in London and finish my studies. And what else? I could not return to Prague. Even were the option available, I would walk through the days in anguish and despair, reminded daily—by every tree, by the rushing of the river, and by the parks and the ponds—of things lost.

The piercing wail of a fire engine, so reminiscent of the air-raid sirens during the war, woke me one night. The sound triggered the memory of the drone of a bomber formation flying overhead, unloading bombs that descended by the hundreds with a whistling sound. Programmed for defense, I crawled under the bed.

I was bathed in sweat, my temples throbbed, and my chest felt as if it were filling with hot cinders. The smell of blood and the screams of broken bodies floated on the ashes of rising smoke. Everything was unreeling and I knew I was back in that time, as if the image was translucently veiled, and ready to spring at me. I pressed my hands against my clammy temples in order to goad the tangled images back to the present. I crawled to the window.and looked out into a street still displaying its rubble in the dim lights of the streetlamps. There was only silence.

I existed in a world of crossed wires and unremitting depression. I toyed with the idea of America, but could not decide anything. I repeatedly looked at Uncle Charles's "To Whom It May Concern" letter, but muffled voices from the continent tore at me, demanding my presence. I could not go back. I could not stay, either.

Lilka and Vaclav were going to Riyadh, Nora was in Holice, and others had gone to Israel, Sweden, or South America. There was only one answer to the unscrambling of the crossed wires in my head: Leave.

I placed Uncle Charles's letter in a folder and walked to the American embassy. I was still not free of past images. The ruins I passed along the way still connected the wires in my head to the sound of a bomber formation and urged me to run.

The embassy was crowded and I was tempted to leave and come back another day, but a young man engaged me in conversation.

"Are you going to America?" he asked, his eyes beaming.

"Yes, are you?"

"Of course."

The door to the consul's office opened and it was my turn.

I sat opposite a young man who seemed totally uninterested in what he was doing.

"Identification?"

I handed him my Czech passport.

He opened it, read the first page, and threw it on the desk. "The Czech quota is closed."

"Which quota is open?"

"The German quota is unlimited, but that certainly isn't going to help you."

I took the passport from the desk, opened it to the front page, and pointed to Cologne.

"You were born in Germany?"

"Yes."

"That's different. You can have a visa in about two weeks, if you have a guarantor."

What irony, I thought. The former enemy of the United States had an unlimited quota to enter America, the conquered Czech did not.

I whipped out Uncle Charles's letter and placed it on his desk. He looked it over carefully. "Looks good. Be here in two weeks."

The day of departure had come. The fog had lifted, and for once the sun was hanging round and yellow in a hazy blue sky, but there was a knot in my stomach.

I was leaving behind everything I had known, good and bad, and I would have no reference to anything where I was going. Should I be leaving it all behind? Was I not tied to the past? Would I be able to escape its constricting hand? Should I?

Lilka gave me the push. "You have no one here. You cannot live in Prague. Go. Find a new world. After all, you have no ties anywhere."

On that warm July day Lilka, Vaclav, and I stood on the airfield in an uneasy silence. The huge plane, a Constellation, sat on the tarmac like some grounded bird unable to lift its wings.

"I don't know why you want to go to gangster land," Vaclav said in an effort to sound cheerful.

"I am going to the land of the oranges." Even as I said this, I felt full of a dense sadness making me want to weep for severing myself from the past, for leaving my friends, my roots. The familiar acute ache threatened to scuttle my determination to leave. I quickly embraced Lilka and Vaclav, tore myself away, and walked up the steps into the plane.

The plane shuddered as it rose, as if unwilling to quit the firm ground. Below me lay a destroyed Europe. Buried there was my childhood and youth, and all that was left standing was an impenetrable forest of sadness. Ahead lay an unknown world. The plane glided over a vast sea where there were no shattered houses, no burned parks, and no hungry people to remind me of anything, at least for a little while. A new life beckoned in a country where the buildings touched the sky and the oranges grew as large as soccer balls.

As the plane sailed over the tranquil sea, the smoldering rage that had begun in Berlin when I was a child fell away, and I felt a sense of peace, something I had not felt in a long time. In my pocket I carried the almost weightless remains of my old life: a cracked and faded black-and-white photograph.

Epilogue

Each spring, when the buckeye trees bloom in the Sierra foothills, their erect blossoms, white against the tree's green foliage, remind me of the chestnut trees in Prague.

It took thirty years before I could bring myself to return. I have been there during the Communist era and after, but I have never gone to Terezin—the concentration camp near Prague where my mother spent some of her last days. The city holds no terror for me now. I am drawn to it like a moth to a flame. I see a beautiful city that beckons me with its Gothic churches, its Renaissance architecture, and its cobblestone streets, and yet I am saddened when I sit on a bench on the Letna or wander through the parks. I long for the distant Prague, the one before I crossed borders to another world.

Nora still lives there. We do not speak of the past. We visit her two sons and daughter. They are Czechs. They are all married now, but only one of her sons has children. Her four grandchildren are now in America.

When Lilka and Vaclav completed their tour of duty in Riyadh, they settled in Australia. Their two sons are the new generation of Australians.

My daughters are Americans, descended from a Hungarian grandfather and a Belgian grandmother.

With each war and each new political folly, people are displaced and become citizens of countries other than their own, making a melting pot of the world, mixing the gene pool. Perhaps, one day, these new generations will have learned something from the follies of the generations that went before.

The legacy of my past is a dichotomy of two selves. One half of me wants to be here, the other somewhere else. Wherever I am, it is the wrong place for part of me. I straddle two worlds, not fully comfortable in either. I can live anywhere but am at home nowhere. My roots are shallow, but they spread like fingers across the globe, encompassing the world.

And the past still lurks in the wail of an ambulance and the black boots of the highway patrol.

Miriam Darvas' Journey From Prague To London

KEY
- • - City (grey dot); ● - City passed through (black dot);
- ⎯ 1939 country border (grey line); ━ Miriam's Journey (black line)

1 Journey from Prague, Czechoslovakia to Katowice, Poland
2 Katowice, Poland to Gdansk, Poland
3 Gdansk, Poland to Gdynia, Poland
4 Ship from Gdynia, Poland to Sölvesborg, Sweden
5 Sölvesborg, Sweden to Gothenburg, Sweden
6 Ship from Gothenburg, Sweden to London, England via Southampton

Please note this map is for representational purposes only and is not to scale

Author's Note

My mother, Maria Margaretha Mathilde Müller, was born in Antwerp, Belgium in 1900. Her family was Catholic and ethnic German. Her father, Klaus, was a ship's captain.

After World War I all ethnic Germans were expelled from Belgium as they were from Czechoslovakia and other countries after World War II

The family made the arduous trip, escorted by the Belgian police, to the German border. They wandered through Germany for a while. I do not know where they eventually settled. I recently learned that my mother had a brother, Paul Christian. His son, my cousin, still lives in Germany. He was a member of the Hitler Youth. I have not met him.

My father, Janos Zoltan Darvas, was born in Tan Nagy, Hungary in 1891, which was then part of the Austro-Hungarian Empire. He graduated from the University of Koloszwar. He established himself as a poet at an early age. During World War I, he served in the Hungarian cavalry as a lieutenant. In 1916, during the battle of Lutsk in Poland, the Russians captured 200,000 men of the Austro-Hungarian army. My father was one of them. He spent seven years in a Siberian gulag. He was released in 1923; five years after the war had ended. Upon his release, the Austro-Hungarian Empire was gone. Koloszvar had been renamed Clujand had become part of Rumania. Hungary had become a dictatorship under Admiral Horty.

Stateless, his family gone, he went to Germany, where, as in Hungary, a dictatorship was developing. The country was devastated by war. There was astronomical inflation. One pound of butter cost a million marks. Poverty and anger against the government created wild strikes. His articles exposing the suppression of the workers earned him the attention of the new-Nazi party. By this time he had married my mother. Where and how they met I do not know. I was born in Cologne. When the German dictator, Hitler, came to power in 1933, my father, because of his political writing, was a marked man. Anti-Nazi writers and Jews were being arrested. My father was both. He planned a careful escape. His route was to move from town to town along the River Rhein to Koblenz and then along the River Main meandering towards Prague. We stayed in various towns a year or a few months in order not to arouse suspicion. My sister Esther was born in Koblenz. She lived long enough to die before we made it to Prague.

The wandering life continued for me into my adulthood. Thus, two generations became displaced as a result of political whims. It was not till my own daughter was twelve years old that I realized what tremendous cost it was to my mother to let me go into the unknown.

World War I started in 1914 when my mother was 14 and ended in 1918 when she was 18. World War II began when I was thirteen and ended when I was nineteen. My youth was not so different from my mother's.

Miriam Darvas
May 2015

Acknowledgments

Thank you to Mark Pearce and Alison Crellin for reviving *Farewell to Prague* and for creating a beautiful new version.

Miriam Darvas photographed in 1948